Note to Readers

While the Harringtons and Wakamutsus are fictional characters, the events surrounding them are not. When the United States entered World War II, people were afraid. Families living on the West Coast feared being bombed by Japanese planes. Those people who lived on the East Coast feared getting fired on by German U-boats.

Everyone quickly joined forces to arm the young people going to war. The Boeing Company, which made bombers, was actually disguised just as it's described in this story. Americans used all their energy and talent to try to win the war.

But because of fear, some people wanted those with any Japanese heritage to be imprisoned, even if they were American citizens. They thought Japanese-Americans might be spies. The decision to put Japanese-Americans in camps during the war was one of the saddest moments in American history.

In 1976, President Gerald R. Ford said that this action was a national mistake. Then on August 10, 1988, President Ronald Reagan signed a law that gave an official government apology and payment of $20,000 to any living person who had been ordered into the camps.

WAR
STRIKES

Norma Jean Lutz

PUBLISHING, INC.
Uhrichsville, Ohio

To Bruce and Becky: It's been an incredibly "adventurous" journey. Thank you for making it a pleasurable one!

ISBN 1-57748-512-2

Published by Barbour Publishing, Inc., P.O. Box 719, Uhrichsville, Ohio 44683
http://www.barbourbooks.com

Member of the
Evangelical Christian
Publishers Association

Printed in the United States of America.

Cover illustration by Peter Pagano.
Inside illustrations by Adam Wallenta.

CHAPTER 1
Thanksgiving

Thirteen-year-old Frank Harrington watched in amusement as his little brother, Eddie, attempted to eat a piece of his Thanksgiving pumpkin pie with his chopsticks. Eddie and Barb, the seven-year-old twins, were sitting at a smaller table off in the corner, while the older children and grown-ups were crowded around the Wakamutsus' dining room table. Barb was stifling giggles at her twin's antics.

The giggles drew Mama's attention. She frowned. "Eddie. Use your fork."

"But why?" he said. "If I lived in Japan I'd have to use my

chopsticks for everything—not just the rice and noodles."

Mama frowned again and gave a little shake of her finger, warning Eddie that his backtalk had run its limits. Reluctantly, he laid down his red-and-turquoise lacquered chopsticks and picked up his fork. Frank was rather sorry the show was over. Eddie could be quite entertaining at times.

Frank was uncomfortably full from the abundant dinner he'd just wolfed down. Mama continually told him to chew slowly, but it was a difficult order to follow. During the last year, his body had changed. He was never able to get full, no matter how much he ate. Dad called it Frank's "growing spurt." Frank hoped it was more than a spurt. His older brother, Steve, was still a head taller, and Frank was determined to catch up.

"I don't believe Japan can ever totally win a war with China," Dad was saying as he pushed his plate away from him. He'd just polished off a second piece of pie. They'd been served the Japanese foods first, of course. Soup and noodles and rice were much less filling than stuffed turkey and mashed potatoes and gravy. But it was rather like having two dinners in a row.

Mr. Wakamutsu nodded politely. "I am in agreement with you. Their army seems to be flagging."

"The Chinese have them terribly outnumbered," Steve spoke up. "Surely the Japanese government knows that. Why, the Chinese could fight for forever and never run out of men."

Frank listened as his older brother spoke. At age nineteen, Steve seemed so worldly wise. And he was terribly good-looking. All the girls liked Steve. But Steve was too busy working days at the Tydol filling station and attending night college classes to pay attention to girls. Steve would rather read a book than go on a date.

"Their army may be flagging," Dad said, "but the Imperial Navy is still skipping around the Pacific free as a breeze."

"But strong as a hurricane," Mr. Wakamutsu added rather solemnly.

Frank saw Alice's face go pale. His older sister's fiancé was a sailor stationed in the Philippines. She couldn't bear to hear a word about the power of Japan in the Pacific.

Mrs. Wakamutsu must have seen Alice's face as well. She scooted her chair away and stood up from the table, asking politely if anyone wanted more tea.

"Mama, Eddie kicked me," Barb said in her whiny voice. "And he keeps bumping the table and making my water glass jiggle."

"Am not," Eddie protested.

"Are too. Don't lie."

"I'm not lying. . . ."

Mama started to answer, but it was Dad who got up from his chair and went over to talk to the twins and settle them down. As an engineer at the Boeing plant, their dad's work hours were long and late. Mama had become accustomed to settling all the disputes in the house. And with seven children, that could add up to a fair amount.

Frank tried to remember what it used to be like to have Dad home every evening for supper. It had been a very long time ago.

Alice, seemingly relieved by the break in the war talk, also got up and began clearing the dessert plates. She was wearing a silk scarf at her neck that Jim had sent her from the Philippines. It was woven in a rainbow of bright, cheerful colors. However, the cheerfulness wasn't reflected in her face. Alice didn't smile much these days.

There was a war raging in Europe, but with the Wakamutsus being of Japanese descent and with Jim being in the Philippines, the Harrington family's attention was usually centered on the Pacific.

"Are we going to the vacant lot?" Audrey turned to ask the Wakamutsu brothers.

Even though Frank's eleven-year-old sister was as big a bookworm as Steve, she was always ready to go with them to the vacant lot to play rough and rowdy boy-games.

"Sure we're going to the lot," said fourteen-year-old Kaneko. Then he rubbed his stomach. "But not until my food settles."

Frank laughed. "First it was the turkey that was stuffed. Now it's us!"

"Let's go listen to the radio for a while," Kaneko suggested. He pushed his straight dark hair off his forehead, but it fell stubbornly back in the same place. "Or read comic books. Later we'll get up a good ball game."

Frank liked that idea. In Kaneko and Abiko's room, they had stacks of comic books. More copies of Captain Marvel lined the shelves than Frank ever thought about having. The comic book competition first began years ago, when Frank and his family still lived at the Fairfax—the apartment house and hotel that the Wakamutsu family owned and managed. And now, even though the Harringtons lived across town on Queen Anne Hill, the friendly rivalry continued.

Before they could slip out of the dining room, Mr. Wakamutsu lifted his hand. "Help with the cleaning first," he ordered.

"Yoshiko has to help, too," insisted Abiko, the younger Wakamutsu brother. His dark almond eyes were smiling as he glanced at his older brother for approval for mentioning their older sister.

Mama looked at Frank. "Where did Isabel go?"

"You should know the answer to that," Audrey spoke up. "Isabel and Yoshiko are in Yoshiko's room talking about boys, dances, and shades of lipstick." Then she added, "And learning the jitterbug."

Mrs. Wakamutsu, who usually showed little emotion, smiled at that remark. "No matter, Lydia," she said to Frank's mother. "If everyone comes to help, there is no room in the kitchen."

"You're probably right," Mama agreed. "Well, the girls can come in later and wash and dry dishes."

Good, Frank thought. He didn't want Dizzy-Izzy, as he sometimes called Isabel, to get away without helping. In his opinion, washing and wiping dishes was a lot worse than cleaning up.

Once the table was cleared and the dishes stacked, Frank took great pleasure in sticking his head in Yoshiko's room and telling the two sixteen-year-olds that the stacks of dishes awaited. Their groans of protest were music to his ears. They had a Jimmy Dorsey swing number blaring on the phonograph. As he opened the door, Mittens the cat ran from the room. Apparently Mittens couldn't stand the noise, either. Frank much preferred a good radio program like the *Green Hornet* to listening to Jimmy Dorsey.

Later, as Frank and Audrey and the Wakamutsu boys pulled on their jackets to go outside, the twins announced they were coming along. Frank wrinkled up his nose, and Abiko rolled his eyes. Kaneko, who was a little more considerate, just tossed his baseball up and caught it in his mitt and kept quiet.

"You'll just get in the way," Frank told them.

"We will not be in the way," Barb said, giving her older brother a shove that didn't budge him. "If you don't let us play, we'll tell Mama."

Frank thought maybe that was a good idea. They were standing in the hallway by the back stairs that led to the alley. By the time Barb and Eddie made their way to the Wakamutsus' apartment on the far side of the hotel, the four of them would already have a good game going at the vacant lot.

Just then, Steve came striding down the hallway. He had his hat and jacket on. "Want me to hit a few?" he asked.

"Would you?" Frank asked. Steve hardly ever played with them anymore. He usually preferred talking with the grown-ups.

"I offered, didn't I?" Steve grinned. Then he looked at Barb and Eddie. "Get your coats," he told them. "You can't go out without your coats. It's chilly out there."

The twins, realizing they'd been allowed in, ran like rabbits to get their wraps. Frank knew he'd been bested. But it didn't matter now. He could put up with the little pests, just to have Steve there.

When they arrived at the lot, they started out catching Steve's flies with Abiko pitching. He was the more athletic of the Wakamutsu brothers. Kaneko was a skilled and meticulous artist.

Steve didn't hold back just because the twins were playing with them; he was hitting some hard line drives. Frank showed his stuff by leaping to snag a couple high flies, which brought Steve's praise.

"Great catch, Frankie boy," Steve hollered.

Frank warmed under his older brother's compliment. He would have caught flies all afternoon just to hear Steve's encouragement. But Eddie, feeling useless standing between Abiko and Frank, kept begging to have a turn at bat.

"Okay," Steve said, "how about if we change to workup. Then everyone'll have a chance."

Frank groaned. That meant they'd have to tone the game down, especially if Barb pitched. He'd hoped to have a good workout. But it'd never happen now.

He so seldom had the chance to play ball with Kaneko and Abiko these days. The opportunities to come to the Fairfax for a visit were few and far between. And now that they had the whole afternoon, they had to play "baby ball" for two seven-year-olds.

It was just Frank's luck that when he was up to bat, Eddie was at the garbage can lid, which marked the pitcher's mound. Steve was catcher. When the first pitch landed at his feet, Frank gritted his teeth. "Good grief, Eddie. The bat's up here." He hit the air a couple of times for emphasis.

"Aw, hit 'em wherever he delivers 'em," came Steve's low voice from behind him. "We're just having fun."

"It may be fun, but it's not golf," Frank retorted.

The next one came at him on his left side. "What're you doing? I'm not a lefty."

"Sorry," Eddie said with an apologetic grin. "I'll get it over this time."

"I sure hope so."

"Right here, Eddie," Steve said, socking his mitt. "Put it right in here."

Just then Abiko strode over from the broken orange crate that served as third base. "Let me show you," he said to Eddie. Taking the second grader's hand, he instructed the boy in how to hold the ball and how to rear back to give his arm the most force.

Frank leaned on his bat. "I didn't know we were going to have baseball school out here."

"Patience, patience," Steve reprimanded. "You were seven once. Remember?"

The next pitch was pretty fair. Frank smacked it and watched as it rolled right past Barb. He tore out for first base and made it all the way to the orange crate before Kaneko helped Barb get the ball in to home plate, where Steve tagged Audrey.

"Kindergarten baseball," Frank muttered.

"Aw, it's okay," Kaneko said. "I think it's kind of fun to help them."

"You wouldn't say that if you had to live with them," Frank countered.

When Barb's turn came to bat, Steve helped her by putting his arms around her and showing how to swing the bat. "I'll help you bat," he told her gently. "But you have to run the bases all by yourself."

Barb nodded, making the red pompons on her knit hat bounce. "I will," she promised. "I'm gonna make a home run."

On the second throw, the four-handed bat made contact. The ball sailed to the gunny sack that was second base and quickly lost altitude. Eddie, who was faithfully guarding the gunny sack, scooped it up.

"Throw it to first," Steve called to Eddie.

But Eddie was oblivious. He saw his chance to have fun. As his twin sprinted as fast as she could to first base, Eddie came barreling toward her as though he had to attack her with the ball to put her out. In the subsequent collision, Eddie yelled, "Out!" at the top of his voice, and Barb went sprawling in the cinders.

Barb came up wailing. "Eddie, you're the meanest boy in the whole wide world," she said past her tears. "You're just mean, mean, mean!" Steve and Audrey rushed to help her up and brushed the dirt from her coat. The long strings of her knit hat were undone, and the palms of her hands were scraped and bloody.

"My knee," she cried. "My knee hurts, too." Sure enough, her knee was scraped as well. "I'm telling Mama on you," she said, making an ugly face at Eddie.

"I'd better take her inside," Audrey said.

"That's a good idea," Frank agreed. He hoped Eddie would have to go back in as well.

"I'll go with you," Steve volunteered.

"Steve, you don't need to go," Frank said. "Audrey can take care of it. Come on, hit some more flies."

"We probably better go in, too," Kaneko said.

"Yeah," Abiko chimed in. "It's almost time for *Jack Armstrong*."

Frank liked to listen to the *Jack Armstrong* radio show, too. *Jack Armstrong, All-American Boy and Young Aviator* was just about the best show ever. Especially when Jack led his school team to victory in whatever sport he played. But Frank would much, much rather play baseball with his friends—and with Steve. He never did really get to show them how much his playing had improved. He was gearing up for a great spring. He planned to help the Wilson Junior High Eagles come through the season undefeated. Just like Jack Armstrong would do.

With feet dragging, he followed the others back down the alley. Steve was carrying Barb as gently as if she were a wounded soldier, and Kaneko had hoisted Eddie up on his back.

As he watched them, Frank realized that no one really knew what a pain it was to have to live with bothersome little siblings like Barb and Eddie.

CHAPTER 2

The Dart Game

The first bell was clanging as Frank jogged up the front steps at Wilson Junior High. He pushed his way through the crowded halls to get to his locker and pull out his biology book for the first hour.

New faces appeared at school every day, as more and more families moved to Seattle to work for the Boeing Company and other plants and factories that were producing war products. Dad said the U.S. was in the war, whether or not war had been declared. As much war material as they were producing for the Allies, that seemed to be true.

"Come on, Harrington," Alan Dreiser called out. "Don't make us late for old cranky Creager's class."

Curly-haired Alan was striding down the hall toward him, with long-legged Jack Kendrick by his side.

"For sure," Jack echoed. "We don't wanna make Creager any more cranky than he already is."

Frank fell into step with the other two. They tried to keep their laughter in check—especially as they walked past the principal's office.

A couple years ago, when Frank was still in sixth grade, he'd not been on very good terms with Alan or Jack. But that was a long time ago. Things had really changed. When the three of them entered junior high last year, they were friends from the very first day.

Secretly, Frank was glad that Audrey and the twins were still attending Queen Anne Elementary and that Dizzy-Izzy attended high school. He liked the fact that no one was watching over his shoulder as he rough-housed with, and sometimes got in trouble with, Alan and Jack. Just because Frank used to get terrible coughing spasms, everyone in the family tended to baby him, and he hated it. Though he still feared the attacks that left him gasping for air, he'd not had one for a long time. The doctor said maybe he was outgrowing the condition. Frank sure hoped so.

"You two coming over after school this afternoon?" Alan asked as they approached the biology room door. The unmistakable stench of formaldehyde floated out to meet them.

"I am," Jack answered. "What about you, Frank?"

Frank nodded. "I'll be there." Of course he wasn't sure. Audrey was always fussing at him that he didn't do as much work around the house as she did, and then she tried to get

16

Mama on her side. So it wasn't always easy to get away. But he'd come up with something.

"You should see what I did with the Erector set over Thanksgiving vacation." Alan lowered his voice to a whisper as they entered the classroom. "It'll zap your cap off."

Alan's two older brothers were grown and married, so he was like an only child. His banker father enjoyed spoiling Alan. The Dreiser house had a large playroom upstairs where Alan not only had the advanced Erector set with a real motor, but also a honey of a Lionel train layout. Tracks, tunnels, little towns—the works. Frank liked going there. Sometimes Mama said yes. Sometimes she said, "I want you right home after school. There are chores to be done."

Mr. Creager cleared his throat, which meant they were to get very quiet or suffer the consequences. Frank looked over and saw that Jack had a Buck Rogers comic book tucked neatly into his biology book. Frank used to be fascinated with the Buck Rogers rocket pistol and the disintegrator gun. But now that he was in eighth grade, those toys seemed more Eddie's style. In fact, he'd given Eddie his old Buck Rogers Solar Scout badge, which had come in a box of Puffed Wheat.

Last year, the three of them—Frank and Alan and Jack—were always "zapping" one another with their disintegrator guns. This year, while they still read the comic books, they didn't play the games as much. Frank guessed that was part of getting older.

Frank tried not to look over at Alan and Jack during class time. The day Mr. Creager discussed *phyla* in the animal kingdom, Jack would mouth, " I file-a, I file-a my fingernails. You file-a, you file-a your fingernails?" It was a dumb little ditty he made up and set them to laughing every time.

Frank was the one who usually got caught when the fun began. He'd already been to the principal's office once. Sitting in front of stern Mr. Johnston was bad enough, but the lecture from Dad was a hundred times worse.

All the names and descriptions they had to memorize in biology class were frightfully boring. Frank was looking forward to cutting up worms and frogs and using the microscopes. But that wouldn't come until second semester. Jack had told them once that he hoped he'd sit by a squeamish girl during lab.

"When we start cutting up worms and all that stuff," Jack proclaimed, "I know just the way to make girls turn green around the gills."

Frank was sure it was true. And he couldn't wait to see the sparks fly.

When the bell rang and they were headed for the gymnasium for phys ed class, Alan said to Frank, "Have you made up your mind yet about basketball season?"

Frank shook his head. "I'm thinking about it."

The last football game of the season had been played the Friday night before Thanksgiving vacation. Frank had very little interest in football, other than to cheer the team on. Basketball wasn't really his thing, either, but both his friends had been after him to join them on the team.

"We'll show you all the tricks we know, won't we, Jack?" Alan promised.

Jack nodded. Frank knew Jack wasn't as enthusiastic about the idea as Alan was. Sometimes Frank thought that Jack just tolerated him as part of their threesome.

"I've talked to Coach Winslow," Alan went on. "He says we need more players."

Frank wasn't too sure. There was something about the closed-in, crowded, hot, stuffy gymnasium during a basketball game that bothered him. Maybe it was the old fears of the coughing spasms. He quickly pushed that thought to the back of his mind. Those attacks were past, and he was fine now. He hoped.

"Want me to talk to Coach again today?" Alan asked.

"Naw. Give me a few more days to think about it," Frank said. While both Alan and Jack knew about his old "condition," probably neither one knew how the fears plagued him. Or about the recurring nightmare where he would be desperately trying to suck in air, but no air came. It was as though someone were holding a heavy pillow over his face. Then he'd wake up in a cold sweat, ashamed and embarrassed.

Coach Winslow was the epitome of what every junior high boy dreamed of being—handsome with laughing eyes and wavy hair and muscles on top of muscles. He didn't just tell them how to do the layups and pivots and moves. He played right along with them.

Coach had them shooting baskets that day in phys ed class. When class was over, Coach Winslow came over to Frank, patted him on the shoulder, and told him he was a "pretty decent shooter."

Frank looked over at Alan, who was grinning, his sandy curls clinging to his sweaty forehead. His look said, "See? I told you so." Frank just shrugged. How he wished baseball season could last all year round.

That afternoon, when Frank called home to ask if he could stay at Alan's for a while before coming home, he tried to think of a new way to ask.

"We're building something with his Erector set," he told

his mother, "and we may decide to use it for a science project."

"A science project?" she said. "That sounds interesting. Well, be sure to be home by five."

"Sure will," Frank answered. He smiled as he hung up the phone in the hall outside the school office and hurried off to where Jack and Alan were waiting for him at the side entrance. A steady gray rain dripped from the eaves onto the boys.

"I can come," Frank said as they tripped down the concrete stairs. Frank turned up the collar on his wool coat. Rain in December could be mighty chilly. Mama would say he should be wearing his raincoat, but raincoats were for little kids like Eddie.

"Glad you can," Alan said. "Come on, I'll race you."

Jack, who was balancing himself on the broad brick ledge that extended out from the stairs, suddenly leaped off. "You're on," he yelled, his long legs spurring him into a strong lead.

Frank knew he'd be last, but he didn't care. He took out after them as fast as he could, being careful to miss as many puddles as he could. Getting his school shoes wet would upset Mama something awful.

When they arrived at the Dreisers', Alan's mother gave them cookies and milk to take upstairs with them. Alan had the plate of cookies, and each of them held a full glass of milk as they made their way up the stairs, acting as though they were going to bump into each other and spill the milk. By the time they reached the top, they were breathless with laughter.

Frank sure wished he could have a train set as neat as Alan's. Every time he came up to the big playroom, something new had been added. There were miniature trees and fields and streams, tiny farms and towns. The big loop of track went over bridges and through tunnels, while the locomotive puffed smoke from little capsules you dropped into the stack. When the whistle sounded, it was a dead ringer for the real thing. Each freight car had rail company names printed on them like Great Northern and Union Pacific.

Alan's newest addition was crossing signals that blinked on and off. Little bells rang to warn of the approaching train. Frank had never seen anything any better, even in a toy store. He was headed right for the train when Alan said, "Look here. Look what Dad and I built the other day."

Since Mr. Dreiser was head of a big bank downtown, he came home early each day and had Saturdays off—unlike Frank's dad, who didn't arrive home until after dark and worked every Saturday. Hearing Alan talk about what he and his dad did together made Frank a little jealous.

The metal pieces of the Erector set had been constructed into a replica of a working crane. The string "rope" and hook were connected to the wind-up motor. The crane was set near the railroad track, and Alan showed them how he could pick up some of the extra pieces of the Erector set and drop them into the train cars. It was the slickest operation Frank had ever seen. Maybe they *would* use it for a science project some day.

Alan let Jack operate the crane, and to Frank's surprise, Alan let him operate the control box of the train. Alan's job was to move the cars and the people in the toy town.

Even though Frank was having a great time, he kept an eye on the clock. He didn't want Mama to get upset with him and then not let him come next time. It was important to stay in her good graces. When it was almost five, he stood up and said, "I'd better get on home now."

"Wait a minute," Alan said, jumping up. "I forgot to show you the new dart game Dad brought home. Come look at this."

Jack and Frank followed Alan to the corner at the far side of the playroom. There, tacked up on the wall, hung a large dart board. In the center was a hideous face, a ridiculous caricature of a Japanese soldier wearing a military hat and military jacket complete with high, stiff collar. The teeth were monstrous and pointed, and the ears were pointed as well. The eyes were mere slits with perfectly round eyeglasses, and one hand held a bloody dagger.

Large black letters across the top of the board said, "Try your luck! Zap a Jap!" A red, feather-tipped dart was stuck directly between the eyes of the Japanese soldier.

Frank thought of Kaneko and Abiko and their family, and he swallowed hard.

CHAPTER 3
Mighty Man of Valor

Frank could feel Jack's eyes on him, studying his reaction. Alan was busy opening the box where the darts lay in neat order, each with different colored feathers of purple, green, and yellow. He held out the box. "Here, let's have a quick game."

"If I stay any longer, I'll be in a peck of trouble for sure," Frank said. "I don't want to make Mama mad or I'll never get to come over again." He stepped over to where he'd dumped his things, pulled on his coat, grabbed his books, and headed for the stairway. "Thank loads for the cookies and thanks for letting me run the controls," he called over his shoulder as he headed down the stairs.

"See you tomorrow," Alan shouted after him.

Frank hurried through the front hall and stepped out into the foggy mist. It was already almost dark. Passing cars made slushy sounds on the wet pavement, their headlights piercing the fog with yellow spears.

Frank knew the picture on the dart board meant nothing to Alan and Jack. Or to Alan's father, for that matter. Just a funny game. It was because they didn't know good folks like the Wakamutsus and all the other Japanese families who lived in the international district, most of whom were gentle, hard-working people who would never hurt a soul.

Frank's mind went back to the time Mrs. Wakamutsu suggested they use her herbal remedy for Frank's cough. Mama wasn't sure at first, since they'd already tried so many solutions. But it worked. It really made a difference. Slowing his pace, Frank drew in a deep breath of the cool, wet air, remembering how good it had been to breathe clearly again after suffering from such terrible congestion. And Mrs. Wakamutsu's remedy had been the answer.

It disturbed him to think that he'd never said a genuine thank you to her. How does a person go about thanking someone for giving your breath back to you?

One thing was sure. You didn't do it by throwing darts at them.

Frank sat scrunched up in the back seat of the DeSoto as Dad drove them to church Sunday morning. Neither Eddie nor Barb could sit still, and it made for an extremely uncomfortable ride.

Frank didn't go to church with any of his school friends from Queen Anne Hill. When the Harrington family had moved from their apartment in the Fairfax on Yesler Way, Dad had said they'd continue attending their old church, which was close to downtown.

At first it was great. Frank still saw his old friends every week. But now, after two years, he'd much prefer to go to the church where Alan and Jack attended. It was a quaint, white, steepled church on one of Seattle's many hills.

If Frank truly had his way, he'd attend the Japanese church where Kaneko and Abiko attended. He smiled as he thought of the three of them in the same Sunday school class. Now *that* would be great!

As he watched the stores and buildings of downtown Seattle whip by the window, Frank tried to think of how he could be the first one to get the funny papers once they got back home. Eddie and Barb usually whined and cried to get them first. Maybe he could get in the front door first and grab them and hide them in his room. Fat chance. He'd never get away with that. Mama would demand that he let the "little ones" have them first.

Just then, a sharp pain knifed up his leg as Eddie crunched Frank's instep with his hard-soled church shoes.

"Ow!" Frank yelped. "Eddie, sit down. It's crowded enough back here without you stomping all over me."

"I'm just trying to see out. I didn't mean to step on your old foot. I'm looking for my friend, Charlie."

"You can't see him when we're a whole block from the church," Frank snapped back.

Barb was tucked in up in the front seat with Mama, Alice, and Dad. Eddie, whose legs were getting longer every day, was sitting on the hump in the back seat with Steve, Audrey, Isabel, and Frank. There wasn't an inch to spare.

"Don't be such a crab," Isabel said in her all-wise, motherly way. "I'm sure Eddie didn't mean to hurt your foot."

"Who asked you, Dizzy-Izzy?" Frank retorted.

She rolled her eyes as though she were dealing with an impossible child. *You'd never know she's only two years older than me,* Frank thought. *She acts as though she were thirty.* Someday he was going to tell Mama about the copies of *True Love* that he caught Izzy reading. But he was saving that for a situation when he might need strong ammunition.

"Hush," Mama said to all of them, but she didn't say it very loud.

Twisting in his seat to try to get comfortable, Frank wondered why everyone always sided with the twins. They weren't babies anymore. They were both halfway through second grade.

Frank had the car door open almost before the car came to a stop in the church parking lot. He didn't even wait for anyone but headed as fast as he could to his classroom, which was in the addition in the back of the large stone church.

Mama would probably scold him later for not waiting to open doors for all his sisters. But he didn't care. Let Dad and Steve do it. Alice was the only one who deserved to have a door held open for her, and sometimes even she got a little testy. Especially when she had to go several days—or weeks— without letters from Jim.

Frank groaned as he stepped into the Sunday school room. Not the flannel board! Good grief! Didn't Mrs. Carter know they were junior high students? They were way past the age for using the flannel board.

Just as it was at school, new faces appeared every week at

church. Shipping and manufacturing had escalated in Seattle as President Roosevelt ordered more war supplies to be sent from America to the Allies fighting the war in Europe. America might not be fighting the war, but she was helping her friends. That meant workers moved to where the jobs were.

Frank's eyes skimmed over the students who were already seated in rows of metal folding chairs. He spotted Ronnie Denton and hurried over to sit down by him. Ronnie's older brother always made sure Ronnie was in church every Sunday without fail. His father was ill, so his eighteen-year-old brother, Martin, watched over him.

Frank quickly moved to sit by Ronnie before the seat could be taken. He swung his leg over the back of the chair, making Ronnie smile. Ronnie's round face and pug nose reminded Frank of Babe Ruth, but while he may have looked like the home-run champ, Ronnie wasn't too much of a ball player. At least he hadn't been when Frank was in school with him in fifth grade.

Frank pointed to the flannel board and wrinkled his nose. "She thinks we're babies," he whispered.

Ronnie shrugged and said, "She's a pretty good teacher."

The comment made Frank wish more than ever that he was sitting in Sunday school beside Alan and Jack. They would have laughed at his remark. And Jack would have replied with something like: "Next thing you know, she'll be handing out plastic rattles." And the three of them would press their lips together hard so as not to laugh out loud.

The lesson on the flannel board was about Gideon in the Old Testament. Frank couldn't see too clearly around all the heads, but he was trying to act as though it didn't matter—as though he didn't care whether he saw her changing the pieces on the board as she told the story.

After praying and leading the group in a couple songs, Mrs. Carter began the lesson. "Gideon," she explained, "was an Israelite. A descendent of those who came into the Promised Land to possess it. But now terrible enemies threatened the nation of Israel. Gideon was terrified of the Midianites and the Amalekites."

Mrs. Carter put pictures on the flannel board to represent the enemy forces with spears and armor. "Those enemies came into the land of Israel and stole their sheep, oxen, donkeys, and produce. Gideon was so frightened, he threshed the grain in hiding. Because if he were found by his enemies, they'd steal all his grain and his family would starve." She paused to put up a picture of Gideon hiding.

"Many of the Israelites were living in the hills in caves and dens just to survive. How do you think it made Gideon feel to have to hide?" she asked.

A girl on the front row raised her hand. When Mrs. Carter called on her, she answered, "He must have felt cowardly and ashamed."

Frank felt his hands go all sweaty as he remembered the dart game with the terrible face. He'd said nothing about how he really felt about the game. The girl's words described his feelings perfectly—cowardly and ashamed. He started to crane a little to see the pictures of Gideon hiding, but caught himself just in time.

"And while he was in hiding, who appeared to him?"

"An angel," said another girl on the front row. The front row was always full of prim and proper girls, dressed in their ruffled Sunday best, who wanted to impress the teacher and show off their knowledge.

"That's right," Mrs. Carter said. "The angel appeared to

Gideon and said to him, 'The Lord is with thee, thou mighty man of valor.' "

Up went the picture of the angel. Frank craned again to see, wondering what it would be like to have an angel come right up and talk to you. That would be pretty nifty. Something you wouldn't be able to tell very many people. No one in his right mind would believe you.

"Why do you think the angel called Gideon a 'mighty man of valor' when Gideon was behaving in such a cowardly manner?"

This time no hands went up. Not even from the prim girls in the front row.

Without raising his hand, Frank called out, "He was just making a bad joke. Like Edgar Bergen and Charlie McCarthy do on the radio."

Laughter twittered around the room, which pleased Frank. Jack would have been proud of him.

Mrs. Carter just smiled. "It certainly sounds like a bad joke to be called a man of valor when you're acting like a coward." She turned to the blackboard and wrote the word "Abraham" with colored chalk. "It probably sounded like a bad joke to Abraham, when he had no sons and God called him a 'father of many nations.' "

She placed the chalk in the tray and turned to walk down the center aisle of chairs to look right at Frank, which made him terribly uncomfortable. Some of the kids twisted around to look.

"The truth is, Frank, God doesn't make bad jokes at our expense. Instead, He sees us as what we can become rather than what we are. God saw Gideon as a leader and a fighter. God looks at us and sees the potential and promise hidden within us—that which He designed within us."

She stood there for a long moment looking right at Frank, making him feel smaller and smaller. "Once Gideon began to see himself as God saw him, he truly *did* become a mighty man of valor."

After an endless pause, she walked slowly back to the flannel board. Frank let out his breath. "Next week we'll talk about exactly how Gideon went into battle to save his country. Class is dismissed. And," she added, "please enter the sanctuary quietly and with reverence."

During church service, Frank kept thinking about what Mrs. Carter had said. Sometimes he felt ashamed and afraid. Afraid of so many things. *How,* he wondered, *does God see me?* Glancing over at Steve, he knew how God would see Steve. Good, fair, kind. Always helping other people. Steve had all the makings of a mighty man of valor.

But not Frank. Definitely not Frank, who bickered and fought with the twins and his sisters, who had horrid nightmares about suffocating, who wouldn't even stand up for his Japanese friends. Nope. He wasn't even in the running.

When the service was over, Frank hung back as the family moved along with the crowd to the big double doors of the church. A cold breeze was whipping in. As grouchy as Frank felt, he might just bite off Eddie's head if his little brother did or said something wrong. He didn't even feel like shaking Pastor Colston's hand. He maneuvered so he could duck behind someone and then slip out the door unnoticed.

But when he stepped out onto the broad front steps, Frank heard people buzzing around like a hive of mad bumblebees. Pastor Colston wasn't even at the door. He was out at the street, where several people crowded around a car.

Had there been an accident? Frank hurried down the front

walk. Then he saw Steve's stunned face turn ashen gray. "What is it, Steve? What's going on?"

Steve turned to look at him as though he were some stranger walking up to him. Pointing to the man in the car, he said, "The guy there told us Pearl Harbor has been attacked. Bombed."

Bombed? Pearl Harbor? Frank knew about Pearl Harbor. It was in Hawaii, where the American fleet was docked. A boy at school named Roy had an uncle stationed there.

"Who?" Frank forced his dry throat to say. "Who did it?" But he knew the answer.

"The Japanese, Frank. The Japanese did this awful thing."

CHAPTER 4
At War

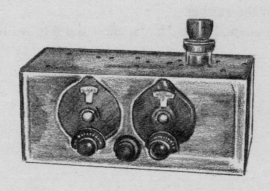

No one seemed to know any details, just that the radio programs had been interrupted with the frightening news. Frank heard words like "Declare war," and "This is it," and "For sure, we're finally in," as the people bunched in tight little knots and buzzed their conversations to one another.

One old man scoffed, "It's probably just another scary radio program, like that 'War of the Worlds' a few years back."

But Frank knew better than that. He felt someone tugging at his arm. It was Audrey.

"Come on. Dad says hurry. We're going to the Fairfax."

The Fairfax. Of course. They had to see if the Wakamutsus knew yet.

No one talked as they drove from the church over to Jackson Street, then to Yesler Way. Alice, sitting in the front seat by the door, leaned her head against the window and pressed her fist to her mouth. If the Japanese could bomb Hawaii, what did it mean for the Philippines, where Jim was stationed?

"What's a Pearl Harbor?" Eddie asked, his voice breaking the stillness.

"It's the name of a port, Eddie," Isabel answered, her voice soft. "In Hawaii. Out in the Pacific Ocean."

Barb was standing up in the back seat, half-hanging over Dad's shoulder. "Why'd they do that, Dad? Why'd they shoot at our ships? Were people hurt?"

Dad shook his head. "We don't know anything yet, Barb. Let's just keep calm until we know more."

The street in front of the Fairfax was abuzz with people. Many Japanese, but others, too, stood about talking, wondering, speculating. What did it all mean? The Harringtons followed Dad as he hurried up the front steps and into the lobby. Mr. Wakamutsu was behind the front desk, his face drawn and pale.

"You came," he said. He had the Philco radio sitting on the desk and was trying to catch what bits of news he could.

"Are you all right?" Dad asked, hurrying over to the desk.

Mr. Wakamutsu shook his head. "I am not sure, my friend. My wife says it is a lie. That it cannot be true. Such a cowardly act. Attacking on a Sunday morning when all are resting and sleeping. But some would consider it an act of great cleverness in keeping with our warrior tradition." He looked over at the rest of the family, suddenly aware they were all awkwardly watching him.

"You come on back. We will have tea and listen for more news." They followed him down the hallway to the Wakamutsu apartment.

When Mr. Wakamutsu opened the door that led into the living room, he called out, "Mama-san, the Harringtons have come." He made it sound as though that solved everything. Frank was certain it solved nothing.

Mrs. Wakamutsu came into the room, her eyes red-rimmed, followed by Yoshiko. When Yoshiko saw Isabel, she ran to her friend, threw her arms around her, and began to weep.

Barb and Eddie, wide-eyed and solemn, went over to the couch and sat down together, saying nothing.

Mrs. Wakamutsu kept shaking her head and saying, "It cannot be, it cannot be. Such a cowardly act. I cannot believe it."

"Mama-san," Mr. Wakamutsu said, putting his hand gently on her arm. "Our guests need refreshment."

"Oh my. Yes, we have guests. Come, Yoshiko. Dry the tears."

"I'll help," Alice said, following them to the kitchen.

Kaneko and Abiko came in then, and Frank went to them, but he suddenly felt awkward and clumsy. It was as though someone close had died and he didn't know what to say to the survivors. The three of them sat down on the floor together. No one suggested they go to the boys' room and read comic books.

Mittens, Yoshiko's cat, wove in and out, rubbing up against legs and then waiting for someone to stroke her fur. Frank reached out to the big gray-and-white cat just to feel the peace and gentleness of the soft purring.

Steve scooted a chair close to the console radio and turned the dial slowly as he attempted to get more news. "If they can attack Hawaii," he said tersely, "we've totally underestimated their power and their aggression. How much are they truly capable of?"

The question went into the air. No one attempted to answer it because no one knew the answer.

They stayed bunched up around the radio most of the afternoon, listening. By late afternoon they learned that nearly all of America's Pacific Fleet had been destroyed by Japanese planes, and hundreds of American sailors were dead and wounded. Perhaps, the announcer said, even thousands.

"The planes were obviously launched from an aircraft carrier," Dad said, "but how on earth did a Japanese carrier get that close to Hawaii without being detected?"

Another question with no answer.

Mrs. Wakamutsu said something about fixing food, but no one was hungry. They all sat in a state of shock. Even the twins remained quiet and somber. At one point, Steve socked his fist into his palm, making a loud smack. "They'll be very sorry they tried to pick a fight with the Yanks," he said.

"I believe we will all be sorry," Mr. Wakamutsu added.

As the late-afternoon light began to wane, a knock at the door startled all of them. Mr. Wakamutsu went to answer it, and Frank could hear him speaking Japanese to someone out in the hallway. Presently Mr. Wakamutsu came back, a grave expression on his face.

"It was Mr. Funai. He tells me many of the men have been tuning in to broadcasts from Japan on the shortwave radio." He looked at Mrs. Wakamutsu. "It is all true, Mama-san. We know now for certain. Joyous reports of victory are being aired throughout Japan."

Mrs. Wakamutsu wept open, bitter tears, not caring who saw or heard.

"Something else," Mr. Wakamutsu added, sitting back down in his wingback chair by the radio. "Many prominent Japanese men in Seattle have been picked up and taken into custody by the FBI."

This news made Mrs. Wakamutsu cry even harder. Mama went over and put her arm around the distraught woman to try and console her.

"Why?" Frank blurted out. "They can't do that! It's wrong! They didn't do anything."

"It's precautionary, Frank," Steve said. "In a time of war, no one can be too careful."

In a time of war. The words hit Frank like a blow to the stomach, leaving him winded. They were at war. His own country was now at war. He remembered pictures of bombed-out cities that he'd seen in *Life* magazine and in the Movietone newsreels at the Rio Theater. Would downtown Seattle look like that? Suddenly he was very frightened.

Late that evening, the Harringtons drove back home to Queen Anne Hill. As they pulled into the driveway, Dad said that all of them were to stay home from school the next day. "Let's wait to see what's going to happen, Lydia," Frank heard him say to Mama. "And stay close by the radio to catch the news."

Frank was relieved. He was in no hurry to hear what his friends would now be saying about the Japanese.

It took Mama a while to get the twins calmed down, in spite of how tired they were. By the time Frank went up to bed, he could hear Eddie's deep, even breathing. He tiptoed in the dark around Eddie's toy cars and airplanes, which Mama was continually after him to keep picked up. Eddie's arm was hanging off the bed, showing the clown figures on his flannel pajamas in the half-light.

As Frank pulled his own pajamas from the bureau drawer, he happened to think—he never had read the funny papers that day. And the silly grouchy feeling he'd had all during church had been swallowed up by something a thousand times bigger.

After crawling into bed, he lay there staring at the ceiling, thinking about the Japanese men who'd been taken away by the FBI. Frank had met some of these men on different occasions—especially when he still lived at the Fairfax. Would the FBI come and take away Mr. Wakamutsu as well? And if he was taken away, how would the family be able to run the hotel without him?

When Frank went down to breakfast the next morning, Mama was busy in the kitchen. As he took down the box of Wheaties from the cabinet, Mama told Frank that the Seattle schools were all closed. So it wasn't as though they were missing any school assignments that day. School was closed. The officials probably thought the students would be unable to concentrate on studies, and they were right.

Steve came over and placed a copy of the morning paper down on the table in front of Frank. "Take a look at this," he said.

The big black headlines that blared the awful news somehow made it all the more real and ghastly: "Japan Declares War on U.S. After Bombing Hawaii Bases."

Below the headlines were these words: "3,000 Casualties in Jap Attack on Hawaii."

Three thousand. Why would anyone ever want to kill three

thousand people? Frank thought again about the boy named Roy whose uncle was at Pearl Harbor. That uncle might be dead right this very minute.

The newspaper also told about Japanese attacks on Guam and the Wake Islands, where more U.S. warships were damaged and transport ships were sunk. Pearl Harbor wasn't an isolated event.

Frank poured his bowl full of cereal and looked at the picture of Jack Armstrong, All-American Boy, on the box. He bet good old Jack Armstrong wouldn't be afraid of any old enemy attack.

Steve picked up his black lunch bucket from the kitchen cabinet, then stepped over and gave Mama a kiss on her cheek. "See you after work," he said and went out the back door. Frank watched as his older brother walked down the driveway to the sidewalk. The milkman pulled up at that moment, but Steve didn't even wave. Frank wondered what his older brother was thinking about.

Just then, the announcer's voice on the radio said that President Roosevelt would be addressing Congress shortly and that the address would be aired on the radio at 9:30, Pacific Time.

"At least we'll be able to listen to the president," Isabel said as she came into the kitchen wearing her blue chenille bathrobe.

"Hurry and eat," Mama told them as she wiped down the white enamel counters, which were already spotless. "I want us all to be together in the living room to hear what the president has to say."

Frank didn't see why he couldn't listen right there in the kitchen, but he didn't think it was a time to be questioning Mama's orders.

President Roosevelt's fireside chats had been a part of Frank's life for as long as he could remember. The president's voice was as familiar and as comforting as Dad's. Today was no different. As he sat on the braided rug in front of the console radio, Frank heard the announcer say that the president was about to address the joint sessions of the Congress of the United States and the people.

Mama sat in her overstuffed chair nearest the radio, a grim look on her face. Knitting rested in her lap. She was continually knitting blankets and socks to send to the war victims overseas. The needles were seldom idle.

"Yesterday, December 7, 1941," came the president's voice over the air waves, "a date which will live in infamy—the United States of America was attacked by naval and air forces of the Empire of Japan. The United States was at peace with that nation. . . . Always we will remember the character of the attack against us. . . ."

Mama was nodding her head in agreement with the words. Alice and Isabel were both in tears. Audrey was solemn and quiet. The twins looked utterly bewildered, and Frank felt the same way.

The president continued, "With confidence in our armed forces—with the unbounded determination of our people—we will gain the inevitable triumph—so help us God."

"So help us God," Mama whispered rather like a Scripture response reading at church.

"I ask," the president continued, "that the Congress declare that since the unprovoked and dastardly attack on Sunday, December 7, a state of war has existed between the United States and the Japanese Empire."

CHAPTER 5
Blackout

That Monday was one of the strangest days Frank had ever lived through. To begin with, there wasn't any school, and because it was a cold, rainy day, Mama wanted them to stay inside. At least, that's what she said. Frank noticed on and off during the day that she would stare up at the sky as if she were looking for something.

Frank wondered if Mama thought Japanese planes might be getting ready to bomb Seattle. He'd noticed how white she had turned during President Roosevelt's speech that morning.

The president had said, "There is no blinking at the fact that our people, our territory, and our interests are in grave danger."

Throughout the long gray day, Frank had felt like a bored, caged animal. He'd read almost halfway through his stack of comic books. Eddie kept begging him to play games with him, but Frank didn't feel like playing little-kid games.

What he really wanted to do was go over to Alan's house, but the thought of that dart board with the Japanese cartoon face on it kept him away. Alan and Jack would probably be in full agreement with the arrests of the prominent Japanese citizens. Frank couldn't bear to hear that kind of talk. He'd have to listen to those remarks soon enough.

That night at dinner an alarming bit of news came in over the radio. "The Western Defense Command," the announcer said, "is restricting all radio stations from Seattle to San Diego to a single sixty-second broadcast every fifteen minutes beginning at 7:00 P.M."

"No radio broadcasts!" Frank said. "Why would they do that?"

Steve came into the room just then, wearing his uniform from the Tydol filling station. "It's so any Japanese bombers flying this way won't be able to hone in on any broadcast signals."

Frank shivered at the thought of Japanese planes moving toward Seattle, primed and ready. Steve joined them at the dinner table, but no one felt like talking about their day. Everyone was worried about the war. Just as they finished eating dessert, the radio fell strangely quiet. The first radio blackout had begun.

When Dad came home from work that evening, an identification badge was fastened to his shirt pocket. Security at the Boeing plant, he told them, had been raised to a new level.

"If we don't have our badges," Dad said as he unfolded the newspaper, "we don't get in the gates. They had army troops standing guard by every entrance as an extra precaution."

"Honest?" Eddie asked. "Soldiers? Were they carrying guns?"

Dad nodded. "They were carrying guns, Eddie. I suppose we'll see plenty of that sort of thing from now on. Protection of war production areas will have to be top priority for the government."

Suddenly an announcer's voice came from the radio, making everyone jump. "The government is asking all Seattle citizens to cover their windows and extinguish any exterior lights for the rest of the night." He repeated the announcement, and then the radio was once again silent.

Quickly the Harringtons pulled shades and closed drapes. They turned off their outside lights and only kept inside lights on in the living room downstairs. Frank shook his head. Nothing was going to be the same.

The next morning's paper was full of war news. Just as Dad had predicted, the government was heightening security in strategic places all around the country, even the nation's capital. Radios on the West Coast were now only broadcasting every thirty minutes. The paper also printed instructions for preparing homes for the citywide blackout to be held that evening and for nights to come.

"What's a blackout?" Eddie wanted to know.

"You saw on the newsreels how they had blackouts in London," Audrey explained patiently. "In case of an air raid, the enemy can look down and easily set their bomb sights on a brightly lit city. So they turn out all the lights, cover the windows, and in a way, they hide the city."

"Are airplanes going to drop bombs on our house?" Barb asked with a quiver of fear in her voice.

"Well, we certainly hope not," Mama said in her most comforting voice. "We'll all learn exactly what to do for the blackout in order to keep safe."

At school, the halls were a hubbub of voices talking about the war. Some were saying how easy it would be for the Japanese carriers to make their way to U.S. shores and begin launching Japanese fighter bombers all along the West Coast. Some students had heard reports of thirty unidentified planes approaching San Francisco.

"There's nothing to stop them," Frank heard an eighth-grade boy say. "Dirty Japs destroyed our whole navy."

Frank was halfway to the biology room when Alan and Jack came walking up.

"What do you think of the Japs now?" Jack asked.

Frank shrugged. "I don't know what to think," he answered honestly.

"I sure hope you're not still friends with any of them," Alan said as they stepped inside the classroom. "That would make you a traitor. The FBI is locating Jap spies right now and tossing them all in the clink. Those sneaky rats are all over the city."

"Yeah," Jack put in. "Japanese spies in Seattle are sending signals to tell Jap subs where and when to land and put ashore more spies."

Frank was certain neither Alan nor Jack had any real facts. But some of it could be true. After all, Mr. and Mrs. Wakamutsu knew of Japanese men in Seattle who were still loyal to the emperor and who truly believed that Japan would win a war with the United States. Perhaps there *were* spies among them. Who could know for sure? That's why the FBI had to be so cautious. As soon as they found out which of the Japanese men were loyal to the emperor and which were loyal to the U.S. government, everything would be all right.

Meanwhile, Frank decided, the best policy was to keep quiet and change the subject as much as possible. As they entered the biology room, Frank saw Roy's empty seat. Had Roy's uncle died at Pearl Harbor?

Frank had finally made up his mind to go out for basketball. It would keep him in shape for baseball season next spring. And it would keep him busy. But more importantly, basketball would be a common ground with Alan and Jack. That was going to be needed in the coming weeks.

Alan seemed pleased when Frank told him he planned to be on the team. Coach Winslow was pleased as well. He gave Frank a pat on the back and said, "Good choice, Harrington. You'll be a real asset to the team."

"Thanks," Frank answered and hoped the words were true.

Jack, however, was strangely quiet.

At lunchtime, rumors flew through the school hallways that Japanese ships had been spotted off the Aleutian Islands. Someone had heard it on one of the abbreviated hourly reports on the radio. It had been confirmed by Canadian officials, they said.

Sharp prickles of fear inched up Frank's back when he heard the news. The Aleutian Islands were like little stepping stones in the Bering Sea where Japan's army could gain a foothold on North America. Then they could launch all the ships and lob all the bombs they wanted.

A boy behind them in the lunch line said, "They're probably building a base there right now."

"Not right *now*, silly," Alan said. "No one can move that fast."

"Oh yeah? How fast did they have to move to slip right up to Hawaii and sink our fleet and murder thousands of our men?" the other boy shot back. "I bet they've had their invasion plans ready for months. Years, even. They've been planning this for a long time. My dad said so."

Alan nodded then. "You might be right," he said as he took his tray of meatloaf and gravy from the counter.

"Of course I'm right," the other boy said, pleased to have someone in agreement with him. "They're like sneaky rats, those Japs are. Nothin' but sneaky rats."

While they ate, Frank kept steering the conversation over to basketball. Practice, Alan informed him, would begin right after Christmas. After-school practice, Frank realized, would keep him away from home more. That would be great. Another good excuse not to have to help with all the household chores or play with Eddie.

To keep his pitching arm in shape during the winter, Frank had created a target in the shape of a strike zone and placed it on the retaining wall in back of the house. In spite of the cold, he tried to get out there for at least thirty minutes every day, pitching to that target over and over and over again.

But the attack on Pearl Harbor affected even that routine. When Frank got home from school that Tuesday afternoon, he found Mama in the sewing room nearly buried in yards of heavy black material. She had told all of them to come straight home from school that day, which really made Isabel upset because she liked to go to the drugstore with her friends after school for sodas. But Mama said that none of the other kids

45

would be having sodas two days after the country was at war. Who could argue with that statement?

"What's all this for?" Frank asked, waving at all the ugly cloth. Then it hit him. For the blackout. It had never occurred to him that there'd be so much to do just to have a blackout. He hadn't read that part of the paper during breakfast. He thought all they'd have to do was turn out the lights like they had the night before.

As soon as Isabel and Audrey arrived home, Mama set all of them to hanging the horrid black material on every window in the house. Their big two-story house had lots of windows.

"The blackout begins at sunset," she told them. "We have to be finished by then."

Frank sighed. What a bother. It wouldn't have been so bad if they could have listened to exciting radio programs while they worked, but there was still no regular programming.

"Let Dizzy-Izzy and Audrey work together," he told Mama. "I'll work by myself."

"I can help you," Eddie said quickly.

"I don't need any help," Frank told him. "You and Barb can help unroll the bolt and measure the pieces for Mama to cut."

"That's a great idea," Mama agreed, pushing her graying hair away from her face with the back of her hand.

Frank ignored the look of disappointment on his little brother's face. He took armloads of the black material upstairs along with nails and a tack hammer. He made yet another trip to bring up Mama's step stool and then set to work. He quickly learned, to his chagrin, that another pair of hands were sorely needed. It wasn't easy to hold up the heavy material, the hammer, and the tacks all at the same time. The material kept slipping out of his hands before he had the chance to drive in one silly tack. He'd smugly thought he'd have the whole upstairs done in an hour. But after one hour, he'd only done two rooms.

It was Alice who saved him. When she arrived home from work and came upstairs to change clothes, she saw his plight.

"Hey, Frank, you can't do that all by yourself," she told him. "I'll be there in just a second to give you a hand."

Was Frank ever glad that she'd not been there earlier when he'd made his remarks about not needing any help!

By the time Steve arrived home, they were almost finished.

Frank, Eddie, and Steve were outdoors checking for places where tiny beams of light might try to seep through when Dad arrived home in the DeSoto. Because of the blackout, he'd been allowed to go home before dark. There was only ten minutes to spare before the alarms were scheduled to go off.

Just as Dad and the boys finished their walk around the outside of the house and headed in the front door, the warning sirens wailed. All the lights in the neighborhood went out. No cars were moving on the streets, and every street light was extinguished. The quiet was almost eerie.

The family sat in the living room, where Mama had lit small candles. They ate sandwiches that Isabel had prepared for dinner.

"This is almost like a picnic," Barb said.

Count on Barb to see the bright side, Frank thought. She was their little curly-headed Shirley Temple who was always the bright-eyed optimist.

"It'd be a better picnic," Audrey said, "if we could listen to *Fibber McGee and Molly.*" That was her favorite show on Tuesday nights.

The night felt like the longest night of Frank's life. He kept thinking what it might be like if bombers truly were buzzing over the city, looking for places to drop their bombs. It was eerily quiet. The radio gave short announcements every half hour, then returned to its unusual silence. Only one radio station was allowed to operate in the entire city.

The Harringtons went to bed early, each with their own thoughts. *So this,* Frank decided, *is what war is like.*

CHAPTER 6
Eleanor Roosevelt

On Thursday evening after the Pearl Harbor attack, Eleanor Roosevelt arrived in Seattle. As assistant director of the Office of Civilian Defense, the president's wife had been in California making speeches about what people could do to keep the country safe during war. From there she was making her way up the West Coast, finally stopping in Seattle.

As soon as Mama found out, she made plans for her five youngest children to be downtown at the auditorium where Mrs. Roosevelt's talk was to take place.

At first, Frank wasn't too keen on the idea of going to hear the First Lady. If it'd been President Roosevelt himself, it might have been different. And if Dad and Steve could have been along with them, it would have been much better. Mama gave them time to wolf down peanut butter and jelly sandwiches after school and then herded them to the bus stop where they caught a downtown bus.

Because Mama pushed them to arrive early, they had good seats near the front and smack dab in the middle. After hearing the First Lady speak, Frank had to admit that Mrs. Roosevelt was as good a speaker as her husband. Her encouraging words to them about hard work, courage, and determination in winning the war filled them with hope.

"We have all the resources needed in this country to win this war," she said. "All we have to do is determine in our hearts and minds to use those resources."

She explained a new volunteer service called AWVS, which stood for American Women Volunteer Service, as well as the Citizen's Defense Corps and other groups being formed. Through these groups, every person in the United States could play a part in winning the war. At the close of the speech, the citizens of Seattle gave Mrs. Roosevelt a standing ovation.

Following the speech, Mama stood in a long line to sign up for the AWVS and signed Alice up as well. While they waited for her, Eddie and Barb both whined about being hungry. Frank felt as though his insides were caving in, but he sure wasn't going to be a baby about it. When Mama came over to where they were waiting, she announced that they were going to the corner grill for sandwiches and malteds before taking the bus home. Mama could be pretty neat sometimes.

As they walked down the street, Frank looked at the store

windows with mild shock. All the trappings of the coming Christmas season—glittery tinsel, cottony fake snow, blinking strings of lights, and round-bellied, red-cheeked Santas—filled the displays.

The onset of war had pushed Christmas to the background. Momentarily forgetting their stomachs, Barb and Eddie pressed their noses to the windows to admire the toys. Mama practically had to pry them off so they could continue on their way.

"Will we still have Christmas?" Barb wanted to know as she slid into the red seat of the restaurant booth. "Even though there's a war?"

"We'll always have Christmas," Mama assured her. "No matter what."

What Mama failed to say was what kind of Christmas it would be.

Before the week was out, Mama and Alice had both reported to the local office of Civilian Defense and received their armbands and tin helmets. Mama was an air raid warden, and Alice was part of the Emergency Food and Housing Corps. They received a schedule of classes where they and other Civilian Defense workers would learn exactly what to do in case of an air raid.

Frank picked up a booklet that Mama and Alice had brought home. The cover showed Uncle Sam saying: "Here are the answers to everyone's questions! The book that should be in the home of every American!"

A picture showed tall buildings enveloped in flames. "How You Can Defend Your Home," the title declared. "A Handbook of Air Raid Preparedness."

Frank flipped through the pages, which showed how people living in London had learned to help each other when the bombs began falling. Picture after picture of planes pointed out how a person could tell the differences between friendly planes and enemy, aircraft. Closing the book, Frank put it back down on the living room table and tried to shut it out of his mind. Everything that had to do with war was so scary!

At school, the students met in an assembly where old gas masks from the Great War were handed out. Civilian Defense instructors taught the students how to put the masks on and fit them to their faces. The inside of the mask had a thick, heavy, musty smell, and as Frank pulled his down over his face, the old familiar terror of suffocating nearly overpowered him. He pulled it off as quickly as he'd put it on. Since the other guys were cutting up with embarrassed laughter at how bug-eyed they all looked, Frank's moment of gut-wrenching fear went unnoticed.

Frank guessed if the Japanese decided to drop gas bombs on Seattle, he'd just have to die from the gas. He'd sure enough die of fright if he had to wear one of those things for very long.

One day Frank arrived at school to find that Coach Winslow had left. Just like that, he'd enlisted. No more young, handsome, muscular, smiling coach.

"Now what?" Alan wondered out loud in a voice filled with bewilderment. "Who'll lead the Wilson Eagles on to victory now?"

The principal asked their history teacher to take over phys ed class for now. The principal didn't seem to have any answers, either. Later they learned that two other young teachers had enlisted as well. More students were arriving each day, and more teachers were leaving. Maybe there wouldn't be any baseball team at all that spring. The thought made Frank sick.

The following Sunday at church, Ronnie Denton told Frank that his older brother had enlisted.

"Where will you live?" Frank asked. "Who'll take care of you and your father?"

"There's a good Japanese family next door. They've offered to help. But," Ronnie added, "I can pretty well take care of myself. Martin and Dad have been teaching me to be independent all these years. Now it's time for me to do what I've been taught. Martin says it'll be my contribution to the war."

Everywhere Frank turned, young men were leaving in droves. All were signing up to go fight the Japs and the Jerries and to keep the nation free. However, at the Harrington house, no one so much as mentioned the haunting fear that hung over all their heads—that Steve might do the same thing.

Steve was almost finished with a semester of night classes, and his finals were still two weeks away. He'd certainly finish out the year. At least that's what Frank kept telling himself.

On the nights that Steve had class, he came home from work, scrubbed the grease from under his fingernails, changed out of his uniform, and went to school. The night he didn't come right home from work, Frank could tell Mama was worried.

"He's never late," she said as she put Steve's dinner in the oven to keep it warm. "School is too important to him to be late."

It was Frank and Audrey's turn to clear the table after supper. That's how Frank happened to be in the kitchen when Steve finally came home. He was dressed in his dark green pants and shirt that said "Bill's Tydol Station" across the back and "Steve" stitched in green over his pocket. His hat was in one hand, his lunch box in the other.

Mama was standing at the sink, so she had to have seen him walking up the driveway, but she said nothing. When he came in, closing the back door behind him, she said, "You're sure late. You'll have to step on it to get to class on time."

Then Frank saw them. The folded papers sticking out of his older brother's back pocket.

"I'm not going to school tonight, Mama."

"But Steve. . ." She turned around, and Frank could tell from the look on her face that she knew. They all knew. It had to come. Sooner or later it had to come.

"I've enlisted," Steve said, keeping his eyes on Mama's face. "I leave Friday."

"But your school. Your tests. . ."

"Not before Christmas," Audrey said, her voice barely above a whisper. "You can't leave before Christmas."

Frank went numb from head to toes. He felt like he was just floating there in the kitchen, seeing and hearing everybody else as though they were on a movie screen. This couldn't be his kitchen, not his family. Not his brother Steve. Other brothers would leave. Not his Steven.

"They're all enlisting," Steve told Mama. He put his hat and lunch bucket on the kitchen counter. "There's hardly a single guy my age still in class. Even some of the gals are signing up. I can't wait any longer. I've got to go. The classes just don't matter anymore." He pulled out the ominous papers and laid them on the table.

Mama pressed the tea towel in her hand to her mouth, made her way to a chair, and collapsed into it.

Steve came over to Frank and started to put his arm around

Frank's shoulder. But Frank bolted and made a beeline for the stairway. He ran to his room and slammed the door. As long as Steve didn't touch him, it would still seem like a vague dream. It couldn't be real. It just couldn't be.

CHAPTER 7

A Different Kind of Christmas

Frank wanted to forget December 19, yet he wanted to hold it close to his heart forever. The entire family was at the bus station to say good-bye to Steve. With a bit of finagling, Dad had even been able to take a couple hours off work.

The acrid fumes from the exhaust of buses coming and going hung thick in the cold air. Crowds of other families, also saying good-bye to their boys, stood around in the busy station. Steve's hat was pushed to the back of his head, and his wool overcoat hung open. On the black-and-white tile floor sat Steve's suitcase, holding his few belongings. The recruiting officer had said that most of those things would be sent back home very soon.

Steve was headed for Ft. Benning, Georgia, by way of Omaha and Kansas City. It would be a long, tiring bus ride. Because of the speed with which soldiers were being shipped overseas these days, there was a chance he might not be coming home even for a short leave after his basic training. None of them knew for sure when they would see him again.

Steve kept smiling as he moved from one family member to the next, giving hugs and kisses.

"I know you'll make us proud of you, Son," Dad said as they embraced. "You'll never be far from our thoughts or our prayers."

"Thanks," Steve answered, fighting to keep his smile alive.

When he came to Frank, Steve said, "With Dad working so much and me leaving, a big responsibility will fall on your shoulders, Frank." He clapped him solidly on his shoulder to emphasize his point. "But it's nothing you can't handle."

Frank nodded, then buried his face in Steve's shoulder. He felt the scratchy wool of his brother's coat against his face and inhaled the sharp aroma of Old Spice that always wafted about Steve's bedroom, the bedroom that would now be empty.

"Attention! Attention, please!" came the voice over the scratchy loudspeakers. "Now loading for Omaha, Nebraska. Now loading for Omaha."

Steve started to pick up his suitcase but turned and grabbed Mama one more time, holding her tight. He then swooped down and lifted Barb up in the air and hugged her, too. He ruffled Eddie's hair, then grabbed his suitcase and moved to the door of the bus and stepped up, turning one more time to wave.

He didn't get a window seat, but they could see him craning to look around the fellow beside him and wave one more time, to blow one more kiss. The door hissed shut, the motor revved, and the wheels turned as the bus pulled out of the station, carrying Steve thousands of miles away from them.

"A tanker ship near Santa Cruz, California, has been shelled by a Japanese submarine and is burning out of control."

Frank was lying across Steve's bed doing his despised biology homework and listening to Steve's radio when the report came in. He shook his head. Japanese submarines right off the coast of California? Were they coming down from that base in the Aleutian Islands the boy at school talked about?

Frank reached over to turn up the volume. The newscaster went on to name other ships that had come under fire from Japanese subs: The *Emidio,* the *Samoa,* and the *Montebello* had all come under attack.

"The captain of the SS *Emidio*," said the newscaster, "called the attack 'shameful and ruthless,' due to the fact that the Japs deliberately shelled the lifeboats."

Shelling lifeboats? No one could be that cruel. Is that what Japanese people were *really* like? Frank wondered.

The Japanese forces had already struck panic into everyone who lived on the West Coast. People were on constant watch, wondering if enemy planes might drop bombs on their cities.

Frank thought about it, too, even though he tried not to. Every time he was sure he'd put the danger out of his mind, there was another leaflet, newscast, magazine article, newspaper headline, or newsreel at the Rio Theater. War news was everywhere! There was no escape.

Frank rolled over on his back, folded his arms behind his

head, and stared at Steve's graduation picture sitting on the bureau. He could still smell the barest hint of Old Spice in the room. Steve had been gone only one day, and it already seemed like an entire lifetime.

When they'd come home from the bus station, Frank had surprised Mama by offering to clean Steve's room every Saturday morning.

"Are you sure?" she asked. "I know how much you hate housecleaning. You don't even keep your own room picked up."

"I won't hate cleaning Steve's room," he assured her. And it was true. Part of him wished he could move his own stuff into Steve's room and stay there until Steve came home. But another part of him didn't want to disturb one little thing. To move things about might make it seem as though Steve were never coming back.

Frank scanned the rows of books on the shelves that lined the walls. So many books. Dad said there weren't enough bookshelves to hold all the books that Steve loved. Frank often wished he were as good a student as Steve. And he didn't hold a candle to Audrey, who was the real brain of the family. It was impossible to keep up with either one of them, so he never tried.

Heaving a big sigh, he turned back to his homework and pushed away the thoughts of submarines landing in Puget Sound and enemy planes soaring overhead.

A couple days later, when the Harringtons learned that Dad would not have Christmas Day off work, Mama had to quickly come up with alternative plans to celebrate. It would be difficult enough with Steve gone, but to have Dad gone, too. "Well," Mama said, "that'd just be too much to ask."

Boeing was building fighter planes and bombers as fast as it could. And the company designed new and better equipment as well, Dad said. That was Dad's job—as an engineer, he helped design improvements to make each plane better and more effective.

"We'll all get up at the crack of dawn on Christmas," Mama told the family. Then smiling at the twins, she added, "Just like you two always do." That made them both giggle. "We'll open our gifts before Dad goes to work. Then we'll have our Christmas dinner when he comes home at night. That'll work, won't it?"

It was pretty obvious that no one liked the idea. Not even Alice. But what could they say? Mama was trying so hard.

"It's a good idea, Mama," Audrey spoke into the awkward silence. "We'll make it the kind of Christmas that Steve would want us to have."

"That's the spirit," Mama said. "Remember, every sacrifice we make because of the war is small compared to what our soldiers are giving up."

Frank kept trying to remind himself of that fact. But it wasn't easy.

Then Mama added a little plus. "In the afternoon, we'll take the bus to the Fairfax and share our day with the Wakamutsus."

Everyone tried to make Christmas a good holiday, but nothing was the same. Hurrying to open the gifts before Dad had to leave. Dad leaving for work while the gifts and wrappings were still strewn about the living room floor. Their once-cheerful Alice—whose mind was always on Jim—hardly smiled. And worst of all, Steve was gone. Steve's absence was like a big empty place that nothing and no one could fill.

At first Alice told them she wasn't going with them to the Fairfax, but Barb begged until Alice finally relented. Probably out of guilt, Frank thought. Barb could wear down anyone.

As they sat on the bus, headed toward the Wakamutsus, Frank wondered what his Japanese friends might be going through. While Pearl Harbor had been attacked only two and a half weeks ago, it felt like forever. Ever since the attack, the FBI had continued arresting prominent Japanese men. All the wives in the area were terrified that their homes might be invaded next. When FBI agents came rapping on the door, the man of the house had to leave with them. There was nothing else they could do.

Mama talked to Mrs. Wakamutsu on the telephone almost every day to keep up on the news from their old neighborhood. When the Harringtons arrived at the Fairfax that Christmas afternoon, Frank saw a small suitcase sitting by the door of the Wakamutsus' living room. That said it all. Mrs. Wakamutsu was determined that if Mr. Wakamutsu were taken, he would at least have clean clothes and his shaving kit.

After everyone claimed seats around the dining room table, they ate rice balls, thin sweet rice wafers, and cups of tea. Mrs. Wakamutsu kept insisting that they eat more, while Mama warned them not to spoil their appetite for their late Christmas dinner.

Frank didn't see how anyone could think of eating a big Christmas dinner at eight in the evening. That was the time they should be eating leftover pie and turkey sandwiches.

"The FBI," Mrs. Wakamutsu was telling them, "doesn't tell families where the men are taken. They can't visit their men. They can't take clothes or food. It is so frightening for the children, too. Their papas are gone, and they don't know where."

"Mama-san, please," Mr. Wakamutsu said. "We will be all right. God will take care of us no matter what happens."

She nodded and forced a weak smile, but Frank could tell she was very frightened. He remembered back several years ago to a conversation between Dad and Mr. Wakamutsu. Even back then, Mr. Wakamutsu had talked about the possibility of war between Japan and the United States.

Frank recalled how unbelievable it had sounded at the time. Mr. Wakamutsu made Dad promise that if anything ever happened to him and Mrs. Wakamutsu, the Harringtons would take care of the Wakamutsu children. And, of course, Dad had given his word.

But now—now that the war was a reality—Frank saw no way that Dad could possibly keep his promise. If Mr. Wakamutsu were taken away and if for some reason Mrs. Wakamutsu were taken as well, their children could never come to live on Queen Anne Hill. Japanese-Americans had not been welcome in the area around Queen Anne Hill before the war. They certainly were not welcome now.

Perhaps it was the kind of promise that was given to make everyone feel better. But as far as Frank could see, it would remain a promise that could never be fulfilled.

CHAPTER 8
Air Raid Warden

Frank pulled on his coat and grabbed his gloves as Mama put on her tin hat and her coat that bore the armband with the Civilian Defense, Air Raid Warden insignia. In a few minutes the sirens would sound and another blackout would be underway.

"Ready?" she asked.

Frank nodded. From the moment that Mama volunteered for the job of surveying the neighborhood, Frank determined she would never go out by herself.

The blackout curtains now hung on big rods that Mama had put up in each room. They could be pulled closed for the blackouts. Each set was carefully overlapped to keep out every speck of light, then opened after the blackout was over. Frank had helped put up the rods, climbing up and down on the ladder and screwing the brackets into the walls. It took an entire Saturday.

In preparation for this latest blackout, Alice and Isabel hurried from room to room, pulling all the heavy curtains closed. Just as they finished the last ones in the kitchen, the sirens began to blare. Outside lights went off, and Frank and Mama walked out the back door into the cold, black night. They gave their eyes a moment to adjust to the darkness. It was Mama's job to check the houses in their block to be sure no tiny bits of light could be seen anywhere.

A filmy veil of mist sparkled in the moonlight and blanketed the two of them in a damp cocoon. It was as though they were all alone in a deserted world of darkness. Soft sounds of the fog horns from Puget Sound floated toward them.

When they'd walked about a block, Mama pointed to a bay window in one of the houses. "See there, Frank? See how the light is showing through?"

"I see it," he said. Funny how bright the tiny sliver of light appeared against the darkness.

He waited at the sidewalk while Mama went up and knocked on the door to let the residents know how they could cover the window more effectively. Frank could hear the lady thanking Mama for the information. Then the light was gone.

As they started walking again, Mama said, "Even with all the darkness out here, all of it put together was not strong enough to put out that one tiny bit of light." Their footsteps made soft echoes as they crossed the street to go down the other side. "Always remember, Frank. No matter how dark things may seem, a tiny glimmer of light is stronger than the darkness."

Frank thought about that. It was true. The light broke into the darkness, but the darkness couldn't put out the light.

"No matter what happens during this terrible time of war, our Light, Jesus, will always be victorious over the darkness," Mama said. "Try to remember that, Frank," she added. "Will you?"

"I'll try."

Just then, they saw the vague outline of a man standing at the bus stop. The cigarette in his hand was glowing. "Excuse me, sir," Mama said. "You'll have to put out the cigarette. It's against the rules during blackout."

He didn't answer, but sparks flew like tiny fireworks as he dropped the cigarette and crushed it with his foot. Mama had been taught at her training courses that if a plane had a particular city in its bomb sights, even the tiniest light could give the pilot his bearings.

Just as they arrived back at the house, the all-clear sounded. Neighborhood streetlights lit up in a blaze of glory, along with all the house lights, as people yanked open the hated blackout curtains.

After a rocky start, basketball season got underway under the leadership of gray-haired Coach Flynn. In his younger years, Coach Flynn had been an assistant coach for the Seattle Rainiers baseball club. No one knew how the principal had talked him into coming out of retirement to take over the coaching job at Wilson Junior High. But there he was.

The boys were still grieving the loss of Coach Winslow. They'd received one little postcard from him. That was all. Coach Flynn told them that no one had time for writing postcards during boot camp.

Frank spent a good deal of time on the bench during games, which didn't bother him too much. It was as though he were biding his time until baseball season. One thing was sure—while Coach Flynn might be an old guy, he sure knew a lot about baseball. Frank felt confident it would be their best baseball season ever. He could picture how his pitching skills would catapult their team to a winning season.

In his spare time, Frank continued to pitch to the target in the backyard. The problem was that he didn't have much spare time. Volunteer war work was eating up everyone's spare time. Every week during FDR's fireside chats, the president encouraged Americans to mount massive scrap drives. "Your basements, garages, and attics have hidden in them the materials needed for this war to be won," he'd say.

At school there were contests for the most newspapers brought in during the paper drive. One boy won a fifty-dollar war bond. While Frank was all for winning the war, he didn't much like spending his Saturdays pulling the twins' wagon and going door to door, asking for old newspapers and magazines.

But papers weren't the only thing that the government needed. There were scrap metal drives as well. Metal was needed to build tanks and guns. Dad told them that factories all across the nation would stop producing consumer items such as refrigerators and cars. They would retool their assembly lines and begin making war supplies. Every bit of scrap metal was needed.

"The Axis powers look upon Americans as being frivolous and undisciplined," Dad said. Then with a note of pride in his voice, he added, "They'll be shocked when they learn how much Americans can produce when we throw ourselves into it. And how fast!"

Even cooking grease and fats in the kitchen were being saved and used for the war. A sign by the stove in the Harringtons' kitchen explained that cooking fats "contain glycerine, and glycerine is needed for gunpowder. We are short of glycerine—short millions of pounds of it." The notice continued:

Before the war, two million pounds of fats and oils were imported from the Far East: from the Jap-held islands in the Pacific. One important source which has not yet been tapped to the limit remains. That source is the used fats from the kitchens of America.

So Mama and the girls saved drippings from the broiler, skimmed grease off the top of soups and stews, scraped grease left in the skillet after frying bacon, and added used lard and cooking oil. All the cooking fats were poured into cans. When the cans were full, it was Frank and Eddie's job to take them to the butcher shop. The cans were messy and smelly. It was yet another job Frank didn't much like.

"Eddie needs to feel that he's a part of what's going on," Mama confided to Frank one day. "So this can be one of his jobs, helping you pull the wagon to the butcher shop."

Frank's opinion was that Eddie could go to the butcher shop by himself. Why did Mama have to keep treating Eddie like he was still a baby?

On the wall in the living room next to the radio, Alice had hung up several large war maps. "Follow the War with Hagstrom's Map of the World," read the envelope in which the folded maps had been enclosed. "Detailed maps of Europe, Mediterranean, North Africa, Pacific, Aleutians."

On top of the radio, next to Steve and Jim's photos, sat a box of flagged pins. Alice used the pins to show where the battles were taking place and, of course, where Jim was.

From the news, the family knew Japanese troops were ashore in the Philippines and that the U.S. military was waging a terrible battle, but that was all. While Alice didn't share everything in her letters from Jim, because they were too private, she did read one part that said: *Always the rain and mud, and the stifling heat. There's the stink of rotting jungle and rotting dead. Many men with burning malaria, many with feet infected from fungus. Constant war with infernal insects, and no hot chow for weeks on end. We are weary. Bone weary.*

The words worried Frank. If the troops were that worn down, how would they ever be able to fight off the Japanese invaders?

Dad's work schedule became a merry-go-round of shift switches. For several weeks, he'd work days. Then he'd work nights and sleep during the day. If he had to sleep on a Saturday, the rest of the family had to tiptoe around the house and keep the radios turned down so he could get some rest. In spite of the inconvenience, Mama liked it better when Dad was home during the day. That meant there were a few Sundays when Dad could go to church with them.

One Saturday afternoon when Dad was home, he piled them all in the DeSoto and headed south. They drove through downtown and into the hills south of Lake Washington. When the twins asked where they were going, Dad just said, "I have something to show you."

Presently, he pulled off the road, and they all got out. "Look out there," he said, pointing west.

"I don't see anything," Eddie said.

Dad lifted Barb up so she'd have a better view.

"Donald," Mama said softly. "Boeing. . . ? Where. . . ?" Then she laughed. "Where in the world is it?"

Suddenly the realization hit Frank. The massive Boeing plant had disappeared. Nothing was there but the streets and houses of a residential neighborhood. It was impossible! The plant was gone. Dad handed his binoculars around to each of them. When Isabel took a look, she laughed and then handed the glasses to Audrey.

"What did they do, Dad?" Frank asked. When it was his turn to look through the binoculars, he was able to see better. The entire roof of the plant had been camouflaged! Camouflaged to look exactly like a peaceful little neighborhood.

"Brilliant, don't you think?" Dad said with a smile. Then he explained to them how the twenty-six-acre rooftop "village" was made of chicken-feather trees, painted canvas buildings, and burlap lawns.

"They made the shrubs out of spun glass on wire," he went on, "and then painted miles of lanes and country roads."

Through the binoculars, Frank could see that there were even clothes flapping on the clotheslines. The roads in the camouflage looked as though they ran right into the existing roads. It was wonderful! All Frank's worries about the Japanese coming to blow up the Boeing plant were suddenly put to rest. They'd never find the plant in a million years. What a splendid idea.

Dad put Barb down, and Frank let her have a turn with the binoculars.

"It has already passed the aerial tests," Dad went on. "Our own pilots have said when they fly over, they can't get their bearings. If they can't find the place, think how confusing it would be to an enemy pilot."

Frank laughed at the very thought of a confused enemy pilot searching in vain for a huge plant and only seeing a peaceful neighborhood.

Dad put his arm around Mama and pulled her close. Waving his hand toward the scene before them, he said, "Now tell me, Lydia, is there an enemy in the entire world who could stand a chance up against that kind of Yankee ingenuity? Is there?"

Mama laughed and rested her head on his shoulder. "I don't believe there is, dear."

Frank sure hoped they were right.

CHAPTER 9
Executive Order #9066

By the end of January, people up and down the West Coast declared it was time to get rid of any person with Japanese ancestry. "They're dangerous," one newspaper article declared. "Remember Pearl Harbor! Notice how the Japs have infiltrated into our harbor towns and have taken all our best lands."

People's protests didn't stop even after the head of the FBI made a special report stating that the agency hadn't found a single case of sabotage committed by a Japanese person living in Hawaii or on the Mainland, during the Pearl Harbor attack or afterward.

"A Jap's a Jap, no matter how you slice him," people said.

Dad called the voices a "noisy show of patriotism that was a thin covering for bigotry and greed." Frank was certain President Roosevelt would never listen to greedy bigots. Sooner or later the angry voices would quiet down.

Meanwhile, scores of Japanese men were still locked up, and their families had no idea where they were.

On February 19, the unthinkable happened. President Roosevelt issued Executive Order #9066. The order gave power to the military to "prescribe areas from which any or all persons could be excluded."

From this vague wording, government and military leaders decided that the "persons" were any Japanese, and the "areas" took in the entire West Coast. They planned to remove all persons with a Japanese heritage from their homes and communities and put them in centers where they could be watched and guarded. They would be moved even if they were American citizens. It was enough if they had only one Japanese great-grandparent.

In a newspaper column, Walter Lippmann wrote: "The Pacific Coast is officially a combat zone: Some part of it may at any moment be a battlefield. Nobody's constitutional rights include the right to reside in and do business on a battlefield." Mr. Lippmann also said that "communication takes place between the enemy at sea and the enemy on land."

Frank knew if he ever met Mr. Lippmann, he'd want to sock him right in the nose.

Still, even after the order came through, Frank refused to believe his friends would be touched. Not Kaneko and Abiko. Not the guys he'd played with since he was a little kid. Not the funny, happy-go-lucky Yoshiko, who dressed in long shirts and rolled up dungarees and was as American as Isabel. All three Wakamutsu children were American citizens. When the government finally took action, it wouldn't do this to its own citizens.

It was fairly easy for Frank to put the whole thing out of his mind, because the end of February meant the end of basketball season and the start of baseball season. And he'd never been so ready for a ball season in his entire life.

Coach Flynn, in spite of his gray hair and aching joints, had won the hearts of nearly all the guys at Wilson Junior High. While Coach Winslow could have played circles around the older man, Coach Flynn seemed to know just the right words to bring out the best in each player.

The first time the phys ed class went out on the ballfield in early March "just to see what you can do," as Coach put it, Frank wowed them all. He'd not even told Alan and Jack how relentlessly he'd been practicing his pitching. He hadn't wanted anyone to know.

Coach had them play workup so he could see what each boy could do. That was fine by Frank. If they'd chosen up sides, he wasn't sure he'd have had the chance to pitch.

When it was his turn on the pitcher's mound, he concentrated on that catcher's mitt just like that target in his backyard. He rocked, kicked, and threw a tight fastball. A boy named Paul, who was batting, jumped back. Everyone stopped what they were doing and watched Frank. He put in another smooth-as-silk fastball, and Paul took a swing—a moment too late.

By the third pitch, Frank could tell Paul was onto him but that he was a little edgy. Determination was set in Paul's face as he gave the bat a couple practice swings. He was rising to the bait. Frank came back with another fastball, and sure enough, Paul swung just in time to get a little piece of the ball. The shortstop caught the pop fly. When it was time to move up, Coach Flynn came out to the pitcher's mound.

"Just stay where you are for a while, will you, Harrington? Let's see what you can do with Jack up."

Jack was one of their best hitters. Part of the reason was because of sheer cockiness. There weren't many pitchers that could rock Jack Kendrick. And when he stepped up, Frank could see why. Jack's dark eyes dared anyone to cross him. The first fastball Frank sent in was low. Coach Flynn called it a ball. Frank stopped a minute and sucked in a deep breath. He shut out Jack's face. It didn't matter who was at the plate, he told himself, the pitch was all that mattered.

Keeping his eye on that catcher's mitt, he released his best, his finest. Jack took a swing and missed it by a mile. There was a chorus of gasps from the other players.

"Strike one," Coach called out.

Whacking his bat on the ground a couple times, Jack set his feet, gave a couple warmup swings, and then was poised and ready. Again, Frank refused to look at those cocky eyes. Aiming for the mitt, he released another fastball. In a swing motored by anger and frustration, Jack missed that one, too.

The next time, when Jack was almost ready to fall over in his attempt to grab that fastball, Frank took just a little speed off and Jack swung early and caught it off the end of the bat. It made its weak way to the left side of the infield. The third baseman swiped it up and had it to first before Jack was even halfway there.

Now Frank knew for sure how well his plan had worked. If he could rattle Jack Kendrick, he could rattle anyone.

When the hour was up, Coach came over to Frank and

draped his arm around Frank's shoulders. "Son," he said, "I don't know what you've been doing. But whatever it is, don't quit. This is going to be a trophy year for Wilson!"

All the other guys were buzzing around him saying what a great job he'd done. So much so, he was almost embarrassed. Then Coach happened to notice Jack's sour expression.

Turning around to Jack, he said, "Kendrick, don't forget, you and Harrington are on the same team. I expect to see the two of you working hard to outwit one another during practice. Then when game time comes, turn loose with everything you've learned and aim it against the opposition."

Jack managed to smile and said, "We'll do it, Coach."

In the next few days, Coach had his baseball team put together, which meant Frank hardly took a breather between basketball practice and baseball practice. There was a ninth grader by the name of Rudy who would share the pitcher's mound with Frank. But after a week of practice, Frank knew full well he was a whole lot better than Rudy.

While Frank's mind was totally absorbed in baseball, the Wakamutsus were struggling to figure out what to do about the executive order. Mama mentioned several times how distraught Mrs. Wakamutsu was.

"If they could find a buyer who was willing to pay a realistic price for the Fairfax, it would be different," Mama was saying. Since Steve was no longer there and Dad was working the second shift, Mama often discussed the situation with Isabel, Audrey, and Frank. It certainly didn't do much good to talk to Alice these days. The news of heavy hand-to-hand combat between American forces and the Japanese in the Philippines had made her more withdrawn than ever.

"But since all the Japanese in the area are having to sell

and leave their businesses," Mama went on, "no one is getting a fair price. Mrs. Wakamutsu told me how they sorted out all of their Japanese items and threw them in the furnace."

"Not the little Japanese dolls," Isabel said. "Surely not all the beautiful little handmade dolls."

"Everything," Mama said. "Even the dolls. Even the letters she'd received from Japan that are written in Japanese."

"But why?" Audrey asked. "Can they get in trouble for old family letters that only tell how their relatives are doing?"

Weariness and concern reflected in Mama's face as she answered. "They're in trouble just for *being* Japanese, Audrey. Everything they possess is suspect. Mrs. Wakamutsu felt they couldn't be too careful. That's why they decided to burn everything. She was so broken up, she could barely talk about it."

Frank didn't want to hear about it. He was sure the order would never be carried out. It couldn't. No one in America would ever do such a thing. If they interned all the Japanese, they would have to do the same thing with all the Italian-Americans and all the German-Americans. After all, the country was at war with Italy and Germany, too.

Besides, his first game was coming up on Saturday. He had to keep his mind on pitching.

CHAPTER 10
Dad's News

Alan's attitude toward Frank changed for the better once baseball season was under way. He laughed at Frank's jokes and continually asked if Frank could come over and spend time at his house. For the first time, Frank felt like he truly fit in with Alan and Jack and not like some interloper. Sometimes the three of them worked on the scrap drives. Other times they played with the Lionel train set. They collected and traded dozens of metal "V" buttons and pins.

These days, everything from baby carriages to license plates to billboards sported the big red "V for Victory." Frank's mama had a sterling silver V-pin that she wore on her dress every day.

When spending time at Alan's house, Frank had learned to ignore the dart game with the Japanese face. He pretended it didn't exist. That was easier to do now, because the "Jap jokes" were everywhere. In the main hall at school hung a big sign that said: "Let's help slap the Jap right off the map with our scrap." It, too, had an ugly caricature of a Japanese face. Frank kept reminding himself that there were just as many grotesque pictures of Hitler as there were of the Japanese.

One day Jack came to school with an official-looking piece of paper that said "Hunting License" across the top. Of course it wasn't official at all, but just another "Jap joke."

"Open Season," the paper declared, "for that vile stinking viper known as Jap-Snake." It then added this warning: "Do not turn your back, as this animal is noted for Back Stabbing." At the bottom it read: "Signed: The Viper Exterminating Society." When Frank saw it, he laughed with all the rest of the guys.

Even the cards in the Bloey Bubble Gum told with words and pictures how awful the Japanese were. It was everywhere, so Frank figured there was no sense in risking his friendship with Alan and Jack just because of an old dart board.

A few letters had arrived from Steve postmarked Ft. Benning, Georgia. They were short, written by flashlight after lights out. He was training to drive and operate the big armored tanks, and the training was hard. Steve didn't much like Georgia, he wrote, but he didn't suppose he'd been sent there to "enjoy the countryside."

The Joes who've been here for a while tell me to
thank my lucky stars I'm not here when the mosquitoes

are at their worst. (best?) Ha ha. I hear they're big
enough to carry off a soldier and have him for lunch.

What he missed most of all, Steve wrote, was Mama's cooking, which made Mama smile. No matter how short the letters were, Steve was careful to include a special message to each one of them.

Whenever a letter from Steve arrived, it reminded Frank of what Steve had said to him about shouldering his part of the family responsibility. The thought made him squirm. He probably wasn't doing anything like Steve expected him to. Sometimes he could relate well with Gideon hiding from the enemy. Frank had become quite good at hiding, too.

Warm breezes off Puget Sound brought the promise of spring. And with the arrival of spring, Mama was on a campaign to involve all of them in spring cleaning. Frank was trying his best to avoid it. He kept getting into trouble for spending so much time practicing pitching.

"The least you could do is play catch with Eddie," Mama said to Frank one day after school. He had his glove and ball in hand and was about to slip out the back door when she cornered him. If she'd only known what a bad player Eddie was, she never would have suggested such a thing.

"Our first game's this Saturday," he said with almost as much pleading in his voice as Barb could manage. "I gotta be ready for the big day. Coach Flynn's counting on me."

"All right, Frank." Mama looked at her wristwatch. "You may practice for forty-five minutes. Then you're coming inside to help scrub the woodwork in the living room. Everyone lends a hand with the cleaning!"

Frank knew there was no use arguing. He hurried outside

to make the most of his forty-five minutes. During their most recent practice session, Coach had spent time demonstrating how Frank could improve his curve ball. Frank was anxious to work on those techniques.

Coach also told him not to work on the curve balls alone, since they were hard on the elbow. So Frank threw curves for a while, then fastballs, and then back to curve balls again. He felt pleased at his new level of control.

Another not-so-pleasant aspect of spring was Frank's coughing spasms. There'd been a big improvement in his condition last spring. Maybe this year he wouldn't have any attacks at all. But the fear never really went away.

Saturday's game was with the Brighton Bearcats on the Eagles' field. Mama promised to be there. It was one of the weekends when Dad worked the day shift, so he couldn't come.

Frank didn't mind all that much. There'd be lots of games that spring. Sooner or later, Dad would have a Saturday off.

Coach Flynn let Frank take the mound first thing. It was a great feeling to be right up there at the opening of the very first game. The first batter was a short guy, but with muscle. If he connected, he could probably send one flying. Frank wasn't going to give him the chance.

The guy's face showed twitches of nervousness, which only served to fuel Frank's confidence. He knew what was important. His eye was on that mitt—concentrating solely on that mitt. The very first fastball left the surprised batter with his mouth hanging open.

"Stee-rike one," hollered the ump.

The batter's teammates called out encouragement to him, but the guy was ready to give up before he'd even begun. Frank had him buffaloed, and he knew it. Two fastballs and then a curve that broke over the plate and down. The batter swung at the curve. Frank saw the puff of dust and heard the pop as the ball socked into the catcher's mitt. How he loved that sound.

"Stee-rike three!"

Two or three of the Bearcats had enough grit to call Frank's bluff. But Frank never let their faces sway him. He knew where to focus his attention. Straight down that tunnel.

When it came to batting, Frank wasn't all that good, but ever since he'd been pitching more, he seemed to know where the pitches would be. The Bearcat pitcher wasn't much to speak of. So Frank's confidence stayed with him as he stepped up to the plate. The first throw was high. He let it go. The second one was belt-high and right over the plate. He timed his swing perfectly and slammed the ball into center field. One of the outfielders fumbled it and missed, sending Frank all the way to third and allowing two runners to score.

Frank had never felt better. He could hear Mama, Isabel, Audrey, and the twins whooping for him up in the wooden bleachers. He glanced over at them and smiled. This was his year!

Coach never did take him off the mound. They trounced the Bearcats 7 to 1. When the game was over, everyone crowded around Frank. Even Jack slapped him on the back and congratulated him.

When everything had calmed down, Eddie looked up at Frank. "Wow, Frank. You're good. You're real good. I wish you could teach me to play like that."

Frank wanted to say, "No one taught me. I had to teach myself," but he kept quiet. Mama was offering to take them to the drugstore to celebrate with double-dip banana splits, so he never answered Eddie at all.

Frank could hardly wait until Dad got home that evening. He wanted to tell him every detail of the game. After he'd eaten supper, he took sheets of notebook paper and went to Steve's room to write his brother a letter. At least he could tell Steve all about the game and how great it was.

When Alice sent letters overseas to Jim, she used the official V-mail self-mailer, which folded into its own envelope. You couldn't write much on one of those little things, but they were lightweight and saved tons of weight in mail transport. Some day, if Steve went overseas, Frank, too, would be using the self-mailers.

That night on the radio, Gabriel Heater gave terrible reports of fighting in the Pacific. U.S. and British ships were being sunk right and left. The island of Java was lost. The triumphant Japanese were through the Malay Barrier and were "ranging into the Indian Ocean," Heater told his listeners. That meant Alice would be moving map pins once again.

The *Green Hornet* program was over by the time Frank's letter was finished. Suddenly he realized that Dad hadn't come home yet. Folding the letter, he stood up, turned off the radio, and went down to the living room.

He was right about Alice. She was busy with the map pins, showing where the forces in the Philippines continued to pull back. Mama sat by the radio, as usual, with her lap full of knitting.

"Where's Dad?" he asked.

Mama looked up. "He called to say he was stopping at the Fairfax before coming home. He wanted to talk to Mr. Wakamutsu."

"What about?"

"I'm sure it was to see how they're doing." The knitting needles made a rhythmic clicking noise as she flipped the yarn over, made a stitch, and flipped it back again, pulling yarn gently from a ball lying in the overflowing basket at her feet. "The uncertainty of what will happen next is beginning to weigh on them."

Frank went to the kitchen to rummage for a snack. Rationing had been the hardest war thing to get used to. Nowadays they had to have ration stamps just to buy sugar. And when their ration stamps ran out, there was no more sugar until the next stamps were issued. It was terrible. Meat, coffee, butter, cheese—they all came under a point system that took an accountant like Alice to figure out.

Mama came home from the grocery store all in a dither for trying to figure out how many points were allowed for how many members of the family and for which products. On baking day, she tried out new cake recipes that called for less sugar and shortening. In Frank's opinion they were never as good as they used to be. Dad warned them that gasoline rationing might be next on the long list.

Frank had just finished his snack of cold chicken and was going back to the living room when they heard the back door open. That was Dad—finally. Frank heard the twins running through the house to meet him. Mama lay her knitting down and rose to go put his supper out. Frank followed on her heels.

Dad set his lunch bucket down and kissed Mama on the cheek. "How's everybody?" he asked, giving Barb a big hug and slapping Eddie on the shoulder.

"We're fine. But how are the Wakamutsus?" Mama asked, cutting into the twins' chatter.

Dad shook his head. Frank watched for a moment as Dad

83

tried to say something, but couldn't. He pulled out a kitchen chair and sat down heavily. "I've never seen anything like it. Boxes everywhere. Stacks of stuff everywhere. They haven't the slightest idea what to pack or what to leave behind. They don't know where they're going or how long they'll be there."

Dad ran his fingers through his hair. "First, they put something in a box to put into storage, then they decide they may need it and take it out again. It's a nightmare, Lydia. A nightmare. I don't know what to make of it all."

Frank figured he could tell Dad about his great ball game some other time. He slipped out of the kitchen to go back to his room. He couldn't bear to listen to another word. He couldn't remember ever seeing his dad so upset.

Later that evening, however, Mama called for him to come down to the living room. "Your father wants to talk to all of us," she said as Frank came down the stairs.

Right off, Frank didn't like the feel of things. He went over to the couch and sat down. As soon as he did, Barb jumped up from where she was playing with her Sonja Henie paper dolls and snuggled close beside him, making him feel smothered and uncomfortable.

Dad took the Bible from the table beside his chair and cleared his throat. "I wanted all of you in here so I could share something. Your mother and I have spent a good deal of time talking about this, and now it's time to involve you as well."

Turning in the Bible to the Book of Matthew, Dad read: "Therefore all things whatsoever ye would that men should do to you, do ye even so to them: for this is the law and the prophets."

Then he looked up at them. "As you know, our friends the Wakamutsus are going through the most terrible ordeal of their lives," he said. "While we cannot change what's happening, I believe it is within our power to make it easier for them."

Placing the Bible back on the table, he said, "After much prayer, your mother and I have decided that as a family we will run the Fairfax Hotel until such time as the Wakamutsus can return home to run it themselves."

Frank felt hot all over. Dad could not have said what he just heard. It was impossible. He tried to gently push Barb away from him, but she clung fast.

"But Dad," Alice said, "we can't go to the hotel every day and run it. We have a household here to run. And the hotel needs someone there day and night."

Dad paused before he answered. "I know, Alice. That's why we're going to move back to the Fairfax and live there."

Isabel gasped. "And leave our *house*?" Her voice was filled with the shock and disbelief that each one of them felt.

"People are moving into Seattle by the dozens every day," Dad explained. "This house is really big enough for two families. We'll be helping the war effort if we rent it out to people who've come here to work."

Alice was nodding in her sweet, solemn way. "You'll need someone to keep the accounts, Dad. I could do that."

"Thanks for offering, Alice," Dad replied. "I hadn't thought of that, but I know I can't do it. I won't have the time." Dad was struggling for words to say to them. "I know this won't be easy, and I would never ask it of you if I didn't feel this was the right thing to do. It's what I would want someone to do for me if I were in Mr. Wakamutsu's shoes."

He looked over at Mama. "I'm asking your mother to give up her lovely home and go back to a crowded apartment. And she has graciously agreed."

"Well I don't agree!" Frank's fists were clenched, and he felt his chest getting tight. He gave Barb a rough shove and jumped up. "You can't let some stranger come in here to live in Steve's room while he has gone away to fight. You can't *do* that, Dad. You have no right!"

Just like a little kid, Frank ran from the room, up the stairs, and into his bedroom. He fell across his bed, fighting to keep from bawling his head off. Instead, he was overcome with the terrible spasms of gut-wrenching coughing.

Later, he had to go back downstairs to the kitchen and drink a cup of the herbal tea remedy from Mrs. Wakamutsu. No one said anything about his outburst.

CHAPTER 11
Moving

When Jim had finished his boot camp training a couple years earlier, Frank remembered how he came home on leave before shipping out for the Philippines. Ever since Steve left before Christmas, Frank had hoped and prayed that he, too, would come home on leave, all straight and tall in his knife-creased uniform and spit-shined shoes.

Two days after Dad announced they were moving to the Fairfax, a telegram arrived telling them that Steve was shipping out with no time to come home. Frank was stunned.

There wasn't a word about where he was going. Dad said

that was normal. Troop movements were top secret information, Dad explained to them, and no one should talk about it, let alone add it to a telegram.

At least while Steve was at Ft. Benning, they knew where he was. Letters went to him, and letters came from him. But now, who knew when they'd hear from him again?

Frank muddled about from day to day, missing Steve and agonizing over the move. Now Dad would never see him pitch a game. No more Wilson Eagles baseball for Frank. No more fun practice sessions with the guys. No more Coach Flynn—who truly believed in Frank's pitching abilities. No more operating the Lionel train at Alan's house. No more paper drives with Alan and Jack.

His world had taken a nose dive, just like a fighter plane that had taken a direct hit. He was burning out of control. He wanted to lash out and hurt someone—anyone. He hated the Japanese for starting this stupid war in the first place. But he hated the government for tearing up his Japanese friends' lives in this way. The only place Frank could get the anger out of his system was when he was pitching at his target in the backyard or out on the mound.

Once he tried to talk to Audrey about the move back to the Fairfax. When they'd first moved to Queen Anne Hill, Audrey had had a terrible time making friends. She'd been a real loner. But now she loved school, loved her teachers and her friends.

Now all she'd say was, "The soldier boys don't want to go to war, Frank, but they have to. We'll just do what we have to."

That sure didn't make him feel any better. At night, lying in his bed, the thoughts of someone else in their house made his stomach churn.

In early April, Frank and his family visited the Wakamutsus to finalize the plans for their move. Mr. Wakamutsu read the latest order his family had received from the War Relocation Authority: "Dispose of your homes and property. Wind up your business. Register the family. One seabag of bedding, two suitcases of clothing allowed per person."

Silence followed his words.

He sighed. "We will do this with dignity," he said. "Perhaps the willingness with which we submit to these orders will convince others that we are not spies."

Frank wasn't sure that anything would change the way Alan and Jack felt about the Japanese.

Now that the rooms of the Wakamutsus' apartment were so bare, Frank never felt comfortable there anymore. Much of the family's belongings had been boxed and stored in the basement of the Fairfax, where the Harringtons could keep watch on it after they moved in.

So far, he'd said nothing to Coach or his friends about leaving. He couldn't. Every time he even thought about it, hot tears burned in his eyes and threatened to come rushing down his cheeks. And the old tightness in his chest came back again.

Although the Wakamutsus' departure wasn't until the end of April, Dad said they would move to the Fairfax right away so they could learn the ins and outs of managing the hotel and apartment house.

Once the Wakamutsus moved out, the Harringtons would move into their apartment and use their furniture. Frank hated that idea as well. He didn't want to use the Wakamutsus' stuff, and he didn't want anyone to come into their Queen Anne Hill house and use their stuff. How he ached for everything to be back like it used to be before the war.

Mama and Dad ran a classified ad in the paper to rent the

house. Several people answered it, but they settled on two sisters whose husbands were in the service. Between them, they had six children and certainly needed the space. The two ladies worked different shifts at Boeing and divided up the parenting and housekeeping responsibilities.

Packing up Steve's books and clothes and mementos was the most difficult part of the entire move. Frank wanted to do it all by himself, but of course that was impossible. There wasn't time. In the end, Alice and Mama did most of it while Frank was at school. The sight of the empty room left Frank with a sickish taste in the back of his throat that refused to go away.

The Friday before the move, Frank went to Coach Flynn to tell him he wouldn't be back on Monday. Poor Coach. He didn't know what to say. The expression of disappointment on his face said it all. Coach had been counting on him. But that was all over. No winning season. No trophy. At least no trophy for Frank.

When the school day was nearly over, he finally forced himself to tell Alan and Jack.

"Dad's renting out the house," he said lamely. "It's so we can help the war effort. There're dozens of families coming to the city to work, so Dad says we're moving back to where we used to live."

To his surprise, the boys didn't question him, even though they knew he used to live in the international district. Alan just nodded and said, "My folks have been talking about renting out a room. They said that same thing—about helping with the war effort and all." He gave a shrug. "I don't much like the idea. Especially if they rent out the playroom. I'd hate to have to take down the train layout."

"Maybe you can come back here on weekends to play ball,"

Jack suggested to Frank. The two of them had been having a great time learning to out-bluff one another during practice sessions.

Frank nodded. "Maybe," he said. But he knew it would never happen. There was so much work to do at the Fairfax, he'd probably never pitch another ball till the war was over.

"Sure gonna miss you," Alan said, shaking his hand and slapping him on the back.

"Same with me," Jack echoed, as he punched Frank in the arm.

Frank swallowed hard, thanked them, then turned to clean the mess out of the bottom of his locker.

Alice and Mama both had their hair tied up in head scarves as they scrubbed the kitchen. Frank didn't see how they could continue cleaning when things were already clean.

It was Saturday, moving day. The DeSoto had just pulled up into the driveway. Dad had carried one of the last loads over to the Fairfax and was returning to pick up the remaining items—and the family. Frank stood at the back door by the stack of boxes that were ready to load in the trunk.

The twins, who'd gone along with Dad, bounced out of the car. Frank resented their carefree joy. But then, why shouldn't they be happy? After all, neither of them was the star pitcher of the best junior high school team in the entire city. What did they have to lose?

Frank saw Dad turn and look toward the street. A strange look crossed his face. Frank craned his neck to see what Dad was looking at. It was Mr. and Mrs. Watson, Jim's parents. They never dropped in unannounced. And Mrs. Watson looked as though she'd been crying.

CHAPTER 12
Saying Good-bye

Dad came up to the back door. Opening the screen, he said, "Alice."

Frank could tell as soon as Alice turned around and saw Dad's face that she knew something was wrong. Mr. and Mrs. Watson were out of their car and coming up the walk. Mrs. Watson was leaning heavily on her husband's arm. When Alice saw them, she let out a frightened gasp.

The twins stood frozen by the car, staring at the gray-haired couple. They, too, seemed to sense the tension that hung heavily in the air.

Mama held Alice and supported her as the two of them walked to the door and stepped out to the porch. Mrs. Watson looked up. Tears, already at the surface, began to flow afresh. "Oh, Alice," she said, her voice cracking. "It's our Jim." Sobs caught in her throat, and she couldn't finish.

Frank's stomach felt all queasy, like it did when he ate too much cake and ice cream. He watched as Mr. Watson approached Alice, reached in his pocket, and pulled out a telegram. "Missing in action," he said in tight, clipped words. "This just came. Hurried right over to tell you."

Alice pulled away from Mama and moved down the steps in slow motion. With trembling hands, she took the telegram from Mr. Watson and stared at it with a look of utter disbelief. Then she crumpled. Dad and Mr. Watson caught her before she fell.

Frank never knew his father was so strong, but he scooped Alice up in his arms as though she were a feather and carried her into the house. Mama hurried to Mrs. Watson and put her arms around the grieving mother.

"We'll all be praying," Mama said. "We'll surround Jim with our prayers. God is faithful."

Mrs. Watson nodded mutely.

"You're busy," Mr. Watson said, looking around at the boxes being loaded in the DeSoto. "We'll go now."

"We'll talk soon," Mama said, as she walked with them back to the car. "As soon as we get moved and settled, we'll talk."

Suddenly, Frank heard Alice sobbing. The sound echoed strangely through the empty house.

"Poor, poor Alice," Barb whispered.

The Watsons climbed back in their Buick and drove away.

Mama hurried back up the sidewalk to the back door and hurried in to be with Alice.

The rest of the day was blurred. They had to get out of the house and over to the Fairfax. The renters were scheduled to arrive that afternoon, and all the Harrington clothes were at the Fairfax. No matter that Alice was in the throes of grief. They had to leave.

Audrey and Isabel sat on either side of Alice as they drove away from the Queen Anne Hill house, hugging her, holding her, comforting her as best they could.

Frank twisted around and watched their beautiful white two-story house recede in the distance as Dad drove out of the lovely wooded hills and the beautiful neighborhood they'd all grown to love.

The familiar sights and sounds of the dock area greeted them as they drove through the international district. The old neighborhood was a sad sight with so many Japanese businessmen having to close their doors. "Clearance sale" signs were everywhere. "Closed till the war's end," said one sign. "Closeout. Evacuation sale," said another. Everyone knew the Japanese merchants were getting pennies on the dollar for everything sold in such a panic. *With no businesses to come back to, what would become of them after the war?* Frank kept wondering. But no one in Seattle seemed to care.

During the first days of school at Madrona Junior High, Frank kept pretty much to himself. There were a few of the guys he used to know in grade school, but they all had their own friends. He didn't feel like talking to anyone.

How different it would have been if Kaneko and Abiko had been at school with him. But Mr. and Mrs. Wakamutsu had already pulled their sons out of school. There was too much sorting and packing to do, in addition to the work required to keep the Fairfax running.

Mr. Wakamutsu taught both Dad and Alice all about the accounting books. Mama and Isabel were taught about the front desk. Frank and Audrey followed Kaneko and Abiko around every morning before school, learning how to make up the beds, gather the dirty linens, and put out fresh towels.

As they went about their new jobs, the horrible fact that they didn't know what had happened to Jim haunted each family member. Sketchy bits of news told that the Japanese had taken thousands of prisoners of war from Bataan, but no one knew if Jim was one of those prisoners. And reports described wretched conditions in the prisoner-of-war camps.

The first tiny glimmer of good news came on April 18. Lt. Colonel Jimmy Doolittle had led a raid into Japan and dropped bombs right on Tokyo! Sixteen big B-25 bombers had taken off from the carrier *Hornet*.

"That'll show the Japanese we know how to fight back," Alice said when she heard the news. "They aren't invincible— no matter what they may think."

It was the most Alice had said since the telegram about Jim had arrived weeks earlier.

One evening Frank and Audrey were with Kaneko and Abiko in the boys' bedroom talking and listening to radio programs, when Kaneko grew serious. "Frank," he said, "I want to ask you to keep something for me while we're gone."

When he was with his Japanese friends, Frank tried to keep things light and breezy, telling them stories from school and avoiding any talk about their upcoming departure.

"Promise you'll take care of it," Kaneko said.

"Sure," Frank said. "I promise. What is it?"

From beneath the bed Kaneko pulled out his sketchbooks. There were about a half dozen in all. Frank had seen Kaneko's sketches and paintings many times. Sometimes they were hanging on the bedroom walls. Some were watercolor. Most were pen and ink. All were breathtaking.

"I couldn't bear to box these and put them down in the basement," Kaneko said. "You know how damp it gets down there."

Frank looked at the books, pretending not to notice the tears in Kaneko's eyes. "Since Eddie and I will be sleeping right here in your room," he said, "just put them back under the bed. I'll make sure no one touches them." His voice felt tight and funny. "They'll be right there when you come home."

The morning of April 28 was sunny and beautiful. But inside the Fairfax, everyone was busy. This was the day the Wakamutsus and thousands of other Japanese in Seattle were leaving. Dad was on the night shift that week, so he was there to help load. And Mama and Dad both decided it was important for Frank and his sisters to stay home from school so that they could say good-bye to the Wakamutsus.

Mr. Wakamutsu hired a truck to carry the ten suitcases and five seabags containing all their belongings. A few weeks earlier, they'd been required to be registered. At that time the Wakamutsus were assigned numbers. Each member of the family had to don identification tags, and all their luggage was identified by the same number.

The Japanese families were being taken to the state fairgrounds in a small community south of Seattle called Puyallup.

Frank couldn't figure out how people could *live* at the fairgrounds.

While Dad and Mr. Wakamutsu loaded baggage into the truck, everyone else waited in the kitchen. Yoshiko was clutching Mittens with her face buried in the soft fur.

"Oh, Mittens," she moaned, "I don't know how I can live without having you around to keep me company. I'm going to miss you so much." Handing the cat over to Isabel's waiting arms, she said, "Please take good care of her for me, Isabel."

Isabel nodded as a tear dripped off the end of her nose. "I will, Yoshiko. You know I will." The two of them clung to one another and wept.

"Frank?"

Frank turned to see that Mrs. Wakamutsu was speaking to him. She was standing near the pantry, motioning to him. He went over to her.

"I show you this before I leave." Opening the door, she pointed to four dark brown bottles on the top shelf. "I fix that for you. In case you need it while I'm away."

Frank knew immediately what it was. The herbal tea that helped clear up the terrible congestion when he had coughing spells. When he started to say thank you, his voice make a funny croak. His eyes were hot. He whispered, "Thanks." She nodded. Then quite unexpectedly, he reached out to hug the tiny lady who'd done so much to help him.

Just then, Dad's voice called to them, telling them it was time to go. Alice stayed to watch the front desk. The rest of them loaded into the DeSoto and a taxicab. Following the rented truck, they drove toward the loading area.

As the DeSoto groaned up and over the last steep hill, Frank saw an unbelievable sight. Thousands of labeled Japanese stood self-consciously among their luggage and seabags in a vacant lot. Around the edge of the group stood rifle-toting GIs. Car after car pulled up, spilling out still more bewildered Japanese families.

Standing in a deep line at a distance from the Japanese stood hundreds of Seattle citizens who'd come out to stare. The sight of them gawking made Frank furious. One man yelled, "My son was at Pearl Harbor." An angry buzz swept through the crowd of onlookers.

In a matter of minutes, the Wakamutsus were unloaded. Babies were crying, and restless children whined and fussed. One little boy cried, "Mama, I don't like it here. Please take me back home."

Frank saw Pastor and Mrs. Hopkins, from the Japanese church the Wakamutsus attended, moving through the crowds of Japanese, talking and praying with them.

Big buses were lined up in a long row in the street, some with their motors running. Over and over, Frank silently practiced the words he would say to Kaneko and Abiko—how much he cared about them and how he appreciated their friendship. This time he really would say it. They were his best friends in the whole world, and he needed to tell them.

The loading started. The Wakamutsus moved to get into line. The unfairness of everything overwhelmed Frank. Spinning around, he took off on a dead run to put as much space between him and the ugly scene as he could. Jumping over suitcases, pushing through people, crossing the street, and tearing through the crowd of onlookers and past the rows of parked cars. Everything was a blur going by him. Suddenly he heard his name called out.

"Frank Harrington, you traitor!"

Grinding to a halt, he faced Alan Dreiser. Alan's eyes

burned with anger. "I saw you helping those dirty Japs. And I found out why you've moved, too. You're helping take care of a business for a bunch of sneaky Japs. You—"

Frank tore into Alan, releasing all the fury and rage that had been building up inside him for weeks. Every time he felt his fist connect, he only wanted it to connect again and again. His pitching arm was still strong and powerful, and he knew how to use it.

Then someone was pulling him off, yelling at him to stop. Frank recognized the voice of Jack Kendrick. His eyes cleared and he saw that Alan had dropped to his knees, his head in his hands. Once again, Frank took to his heels. He ran and ran and ran until his breath was coming in ragged spurts and he was forced to slow down. Then he walked all the way back to the Fairfax. Rubbing his knuckles, he kept thinking how good it felt to slam into Alan and to shut him up.

CHAPTER 13
Model Planes

Sullenly, Frank went about his work at the hotel. Work, work, work. That's about all they did. Sweeping, scrubbing, stripping beds, making beds, folding linens, and doing tons of laundry. Lightbulbs had to be changed, rugs shaken out, sinks unplugged. It went on and on.

The hotel side of the Fairfax demanded the most. People were always coming and going. Even Mama was beginning to look weary and worn.

But it wasn't just the work that bothered Frank. He missed his old school and his old friends something awful. Even Alan. He felt bad for throwing all those punches, in spite of the terrible things Alan had said to him.

When Mama and Dad found out that Frank had beaten up on Alan, they were pretty put out with him. "Don't we have enough bad things happening all around us without your adding to it?" Dad asked with a pained look in his eyes, a look that made Frank feel like a first-class chump.

"What difference does it make if I get in a fight?" he'd said, acting like none of it mattered. "The whole world's fighting."

"Your attitude," Mama said softly, "should be that since the whole world is fighting, I certainly don't want to add any more to it."

Then Dad added, "I know you're angry, Son. But hurting others is not God's way of solving the matter. Hitting Alan didn't relieve one bit of the pain the Wakamutsu family is experiencing."

In the end, Frank had to call the Dreisers and apologize, not only to Alan, but to Mr. and Mrs. Dreiser as well. It was tough. Really tough. He'd stumbled all over himself. Then he had to write a letter to Alan, and the letter had to be okayed by Mama and Dad. After that, his radio was taken away for a whole week. It was more punishment than Frank had had in a very long time.

Now that they were living in the vacated Wakamutsus' apartment, Frank and Eddie were in a very small room together, with Eddie sleeping in the top bunk. Frank had always shared a room with Eddie, but having the second grader right above him drove him nutty. Eddie thought it was funny to bounce and rock the bed or hang over the edge and look down at Frank.

Every night, after Eddie finally fell sleep, Frank would lie there thinking about Kaneko and Abiko and how he'd run away at the time when he'd wanted so much to comfort them. He'd botched an important moment, and he'd never be able to make it right again. He was like Gideon hiding away. Only there was no angel insisting that Frank was a mighty man of valor. Even if there had been, he wouldn't have believed a word of it.

Madrona School paled in comparison with Wilson. Dad said it was because Wilson in Queen Anne Hill had a bigger share of tax money to spend. It must have been true, because they had all the best sports equipment and the nicest playing fields, in addition to having a top-notch school building.

The only redeeming factor at Madrona was a shop class Frank had been forced to take. The teacher, Mr. Wickard, was a kindly old gray-haired guy with a pair of small glasses sitting on his nose. He peered over them to look at the students with twinkling blue eyes. Like Coach Flynn, he'd come out of retirement when the younger men began enlisting and leaving their teaching jobs. Mr. Wickard not only made the class enjoyable, he praised Frank's skills.

Frank learned that he had a knack for measuring, cutting, and fitting pieces of wood together. Although he couldn't quite explain it, walking into a room filled with the aroma of cut wood and sawdust gave him a good feeling that he couldn't find anywhere else these days. He enjoyed losing himself in the woodworking projects and looked forward to the class. The boy from his Sunday school class, Ronnie Denton, was in the class, but Frank didn't say much to him.

He still didn't feel like talking to anybody.

The first letters that arrived from the Wakamutsus postmarked from Puyallup, Washington, were full of attempts at being cheerful and optimistic, but it wasn't hard to read between the lines.

Their home at the fairgrounds was in the animal barns in whitewashed stalls. In Frank's letter from Kaneko, he told about their strange, new life.

Nothing anyone can do could ever get the smell out of this place. It will forever reek of manure. Each family has a stall. The mattresses are filled with straw, which makes us feel like we are cowboys living on a ranch. I guess they will get more comfortable after we get used to them.

And while Abiko and I can pretend we're cowboys, it's not that easy for Yoshiko and Mama.

The latrines are a long walk from where our "home" is located. It's not a good idea to have to go to the bathroom in the middle of the night.

Mama was shocked when she found out the shower stalls had no doors on them. Yoshiko has agreed to always be with Mama to hold up a sheet so Mama can have her privacy.

But the mess hall is even farther away. By the time we get there, the lines are long, and we stand and wait. Mama gets awful tired. The food is okay, I guess. Just that there's not much of it. When Pastor and Mrs. Hopkins came and brought fruit and cookies, you'd have thought they were handing out hundred

103

dollar bills. I never thought I'd be so glad to see an
orange!

I don't know how Mama did it, but she sneaked in
with a hot plate in her suitcase. We have it plugged
into our lone little light socket, and at least Mama
can fix a pot of tea.

After reading the letter, Frank felt like crying. Here he was, sleeping in Kaneko's bed, and they were sleeping on straw mattresses. How could anything be more unfair?

That evening at dinner, Frank said, "Remember how Kaneko mentioned how much they liked the fruit the pastor and his wife took to them?"

Mama nodded.

"Why don't we fix up a box of goodies every week and send them to the Wakamutsus?" Frank asked.

"That's a great idea," Isabel exclaimed.

The whole family spent the rest of the evening planning their box for that week. Mama called Mrs. Hopkins, and the pastor's wife agreed to pick up a box from the Harringtons every Friday night before she and her husband left for Puyallup.

That night Frank slept a little better. At least he was doing something to make the Wakamutsus' lives a little easier.

One day when Frank walked into the shop class, Mr. Wickard had something new laid out on the tables. It looked like large sheets of black plastic, about the thickness of a phonograph record.

When all the boys were at their work tables, Mr. Wickard explained what the plastic was for.

"The military has put out a call for model airplanes," he

explained, looking intently at them over his small glasses. "Aircraft identification is vital not only for our soldiers, but for our Civilian Defense workers as well."

He held up several pages of specifications for the scale model planes. "We'll be working with these specs that have come straight from the office of the U.S. Navy Bureau of Aeronautics in Washington, D.C."

A wave of excited whispers swept the room. Frank was impressed. This seemed to be something important. "Vital," Mr. Wickard had called it.

"No one will be forced to take on these projects. They will not be easy. The requirements for accuracy are very precise. Some of you might want to stay with woodworking. The choice is yours."

Frank knew immediately that he would be building model airplanes.

"Only the best," Mr. Wickard added, "will wind up hanging in the Allied war briefing centers around the world."

A boy at a table near Frank raised his hand and said, "Mr. Wickard, school will be out in just a few weeks. We won't have time to get many of these finished, will we?"

"Glad you mentioned that, Ralph. Since the military indicated they need an unlimited supply, I've talked to the principal about keeping the shop open all summer so we can keep this work going. I feel it's that important."

Frank smiled. It was the first thing he'd had to look forward to in a long time.

They began that day learning how to cut the plastic and assemble the pieces exactly according to the specs. Wings had to be tapered just right, and the tail fins inserted at the correct angle. Calipers in hand, they measured every dimension possible to achieve perfection. Even the math didn't bother Frank, and math was one of his worst subjects.

As they were leaving shop class one day, Ronnie stopped him and said, "A few of us guys are forming a summer baseball team. Feinstein's Hardware has offered to be our sponsor. Wondered if you'd like to come out and join us."

Frank shook his head. "Naw. I'm not interested." He knew Ronnie wasn't much of a player. If all the players were like him, he sure enough wasn't interested. Who wanted to be on some cut-rate team sponsored by a hardware store?

"It's just for fun," Ronnie added, evidently not wanting to take no for an answer.

Again Frank shook his head. "I'm not your man."

"I thought you used to tell me in Sunday school class that you were a pretty good pitcher. Were you stretching it a little? Come on and show us what you can do."

The remark rubbed Frank the wrong way. Turning to Ronnie, he said, "I don't need to show *anyone* what I can do." And with that he stomped off.

He hadn't meant to be rude, but baseball was such a soft spot with him now. He ached to get back into top form. Ached to be practicing with the guys at Wilson. And ached to be back in his own backyard with his faithful target that had helped him sharpen his skills. Most of the time he could ignore all of it and pretend it didn't matter. But just the mention of baseball brought the pain up again—all fresh and new.

The next day, Ronnie was absent. As Frank and the other guys gathered around the tables in shop class, he heard someone ask Mr. Wickard where Ronnie was.

"His father's sick again. He's the only one there to take care of him," Mr. Wickard explained.

Then Frank remembered something Ronnie had said about a Japanese family who helped take care of him. That family was probably at Puyallup with all the rest of the interned Japanese. Frank felt doubly bad for having been so rude.

CHAPTER 14

Scrap Drives and Rationing

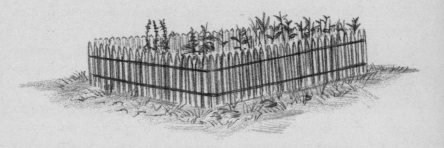

Letters from Steve arrived from England. The letters boosted the spirits of everyone in the family. Just hearing from him made the family seem whole again. He loved the beautiful English countryside, he told them. "Much better than Georgia!" Frank read the letters over and over, trying to picture Steve's smiling face as he did so.

By the time school was out in May, people were being warned to cut back on driving to conserve tires and gasoline. Since they lived so close to Boeing, Dad took the bus. The

DeSoto was parked in the alley behind the Fairfax and seldom taken anywhere.

In early June, newspapers announced the first good news in the war.

"At last!" exclaimed Dad as he studied the morning paper while eating breakfast.

"What?" Frank asked, walking over to the counter to pour himself some cereal.

"Look at these headlines," Dad said, holding up the paper. Frank looked and a smile crossed his face. The headlines screamed that American forces had held Midway, an island in the Pacific Ocean. American dive-bombers had attacked the decks of Japanese carriers that were loaded with fighter planes.

"That's great!" Frank exclaimed. "It's been six months since that attack on Pearl Harbor, and at last we've won something."

"Yes," Dad agreed as he got up to catch the bus for work. "Now let's pray we can build on this victory."

All the news wasn't good, however. The radio soon reported Japanese subs firing on Ft. Stevens, a military post on the coast of Oregon, just across the Columbia River from Washington State. When Frank heard the news, he bit his lower lip. Americans may have won the Battle of Midway, but the Japanese still ruled the Pacific. It was scary. They were close enough to attack the United States. Newscaster Gabriel Heater told listeners it was the first foreign attack on a U.S. military post on the mainland since the War of 1812.

A couple days later, two torpedoes barely missed a tanker near the southern coast of Oregon. Too close to Seattle for comfort, Frank thought.

Sometimes Frank would just stare at Alice's war map. Looking at the whole world, and then looking at the tiny country of Japan, he would shake his head. How could such a little country cause so much terror and destruction? Then he would wonder what might happen if they really won. Dad said they never could win, but Frank still couldn't help wondering. After all, they were allied with the Germans. And the Germans sure seemed to be winning. Their U-boats were even sinking ships only thirty miles out from New York Harbor.

In one of his fireside chats, President Roosevelt told the nation that rubber was needed more than paper or scrap metal. Massive drives were set in motion to gather rubber, whether it was in the form of old tires or old toys. Rubber was so scarce that it was against the law to own any tires that weren't being used on a vehicle. Any extra tires needed to be used for the war effort.

Frank got together with some of the boys he worked with in the summer shop class and went from door to door gathering scrap rubber. Eddie asked to be able to go with them, but Frank said no. "These are my friends," he told Eddie. "You get together with your own friends."

It was sort of a dumb thing to say. Frank wasn't really friends with any of them. Ronnie Denton was in the group that went on the drive, but he ignored Frank. In fact, he'd said very little to Frank since the day they'd talked about the baseball team. Although Frank still felt bad for his rudeness, he couldn't think of anything to say to fix it.

Trucks gathered at the school to carry away all the piles of scrap rubber that the students had gathered. On the side of one truck was a big sign that said: *When you think of rationing. . . Remember what our boys are doing* with *those things we are doing* without!

Yet another sign on another truck said: *Search your attic; search your cellar. We've all done well, but let's do weller!*

Frank was beginning to see purpose in all the drives, and even though he hated the sugar shortage most of all, he could see the reason for the rationing as well. Shoes were added to the list, and now a person had to have a certain number of ration stamps just to buy a pair of shoes. Mama wondered out loud what they would do about school shoes in the fall.

Alice and Dad went over the books at the end of June and announced that the Fairfax was doing well enough so that they could hire two housekeepers. Everyone in the family heaved a big sigh of relief. Perhaps Dad could see how tired they all were. Especially Mama. She had continued to do her volunteer work in addition to all the work involved in the hotel.

Dad complimented them for all their hard work. "You're a great team," he told them. "Because of your hard work and sacrifice, the Wakamutsus will return home to a thriving business!"

Mama and Isabel immediately made up a new work chart. The first thing Frank planned to do with his extra time was set up a new pitching target in the vacant lot. He'd been thinking a lot about baseball. Sometimes he found himself wishing he were playing this summer, even if only with the Feinstein Hardware team.

The new target wasn't as good as the old one, but it would have to do. And it wasn't as private, either. The wide open vacant lot was much different than their secluded backyard in Queen Anne Hills.

Eddie trailed along asking to play catch. Sometimes Frank would stop practice and throw a few to Eddie, but not often. Frank would have to work hard to get his arm back to where it was before they moved last April. It was going to take time, work, and serious concentration.

The boys who worked on the plane models met in the shop classroom three afternoons a week. By now, several of Frank's models had been accepted by the military, which was quite an honor. Mr. Wickard bragged about his prize pupil and asked Frank to help the other guys with their projects.

There was so much work to do, that Mr. Wickard allowed the boys to take home the pieces and work on them between class sessions. Space in Frank's room to work on the models was minimal, but he made do on the small desk in the corner.

One morning, Mama and the girls had gone to do volunteer work at the Red Cross Center. Eddie announced he was staying home. He didn't like to roll bandages, he said. Frank was working on one of the more difficult models, a Japanese Sento KI-001 fighter. He'd patiently worked to fasten the tiny tail wheel at the precise angle. Just as he thought he had it placed perfectly, Alice asked him to come help.

"I need you to watch the front desk," she told him, "while I show a vacant apartment to an interested family."

Heaving a frustrated sigh, Frank left his special project to follow Alice down the long hallways to the lobby. There was nothing to do at the front desk. He just sat there watching people come and go until Alice finally came back to relieve him.

"Thanks," she told him. "I wouldn't have bothered you, but everyone else is gone, and Dad said we needed to get that apartment rented out as soon as possible."

"Did they want it?"

"I think so." She walked into the office and sat back down at her desk. Alice spent hours handling all the details of the business end of the Fairfax. Frank wondered sometimes if she worked so hard just to keep from thinking about where Jim might be, and whether or not he was even alive.

"They said there weren't many apartments to choose from in the city these days."

Frank was in a hurry to get back to his project so he just nodded and then excused himself. When he got back to his room, he opened the door. Eddie sat at the desk. In one hand was the tube of glue, in the other hand was the tiny tail wheel.

"What in blue blazes do you think you're doing?" Frank demanded.

"I was just helping," Eddie said in a small voice, his eyes wide.

"When I need your help, I'll ask for it. Don't you know these are intricately put together. Now look what you've done. You've ruined it. I had that tail wheel on just right!"

Eddie scooted the chair back and stood up to get out of Frank's way. "It just fell off," he said in a small voice.

"You've got your own things to play with, Eddie. Now keep your grubby mitts off mine! You hear me?"

"I'm sorry." Eddie inched toward the door. "I didn't mean to hurt your old stuff." The door slammed, and Frank could hear his brother's feet running down the hallway.

Still upset, Frank sat down at the desk and surveyed the damage done. There was glue here and there, which he was able to get cleaned up with solvent. Then, as carefully as he could, he put the tail wheel into the fuselage at the precise angle, measuring again and again with the calipers.

Once the tail wheel was in and secured, the room suddenly seemed very quiet. Too quiet. Over and over, Frank thought of the harsh words he'd hurled at his little brother. What would Steve say if he could have heard how Frank acted?

Lifting the airplane and inspecting it from every angle,

THE AMERICAN ADVENTURE

Frank suddenly realized that that one model plane wasn't worth hurting Eddie. What had gotten into him? Why was he so angry all the time? He'd better go find Eddie and apologize. Right now.

But Eddie was nowhere to be found.

Chapter 15

New Tenants

Frank was a little miffed at first. He looked in the living room, the kitchen, the kitchen pantry, and then checked the girls' bedrooms and even Mama and Dad's bedroom. No Eddie. Then he thought of Alice. Eddie was probably down in the office, pouring out his troubles to his big sister.

As nonchalantly as possible, Frank strolled into the lobby, glancing around to see if Eddie were there. Sticking his head into the office, he said, "Eddie in here?"

Alice shook her head and kept typing a letter. "Not in here." Then she looked up. "Everything okay?"

"Sure."

"Well, this is kind of different."

"What do you mean?"

"You're usually trying to get away from Eddie—not trying to find him."

Frank winced inwardly. "If he comes by here, tell him I'm looking for him, will you?"

Alice nodded and went back to her work. Frank hurried away to continue the search.

After about twenty minutes, he was beginning to get scared. He'd checked the alley and up and down the front street. What would Mama say when she found out what he'd done?

As he came back inside from checking the alley a second time, he passed by the laundry room. Peering in the door, he realized there was one place he'd not looked. The supply closet. As he neared the closet, he could hear sniffling.

Slowly he opened the door. Eddie was on the floor among the dust mops and brooms, his knees tucked up and his head down, trembling from having cried so hard.

Eddie looked up with red-rimmed puffy eyes. "I'm sorry, Frank. I didn't mean to hurt anything. I just wanted to help." He made a little hiccup. "I was gonna prove to you that I could help."

Frank shoved the mops over, sat down, and pulled Eddie over to him in a big hug. "I'm the one who's sorry, Eddie. I. . ." He swallowed hard and stammered a bit. "I've not been a very good brother. . . ."

Suddenly all the things Frank had been feeling spilled out. He started crying like he hadn't cried in years. That started Eddie crying again.

When the flood of tears finally subsided, and Frank had pulled his handkerchief out and shared it with his little brother, he stood up. Reaching down to help Eddie up, he said, "Let's go put cold water on our faces. Then what say we go to the lot and play a good game of catch?"

"Honest?" The shock registered on Eddie's face. "You really mean it?"

"I really *really* mean it."

"Boy, oh boy! Will you show me how to throw fast like you do?"

"I sure will. I'll show you every trick I know and then some."

Eddie laughed as he followed Frank down the hallway to their apartment.

That evening Frank told Mama he wanted to talk with her about something in private. They went into his parents' bedroom and sat on the edge of the bed. Then Frank told her all about what had happened. Mama listened carefully as he described what happened. He even told her about how he had broken down and cried.

"I'm glad you wanted to tell me, Frank," she said when he was finished. "You did the right thing. Now you see how destructive uncontrolled anger can be."

"I don't want to be hurting people like this anymore," he said.

She nodded. "I believe you." She put her arms around him and held him close, just as though he were still a little kid. The tears threatened to flow again. It had been a long time since she'd had time to hug him.

"Let me tell you some things that happened to me and my

117

family during the last war," Mama said.

"There were no Japanese to be angry with in those days," Mama said. "All the anger was directed at the Germans. And since my name was Schmidt, that meant me. Along with your aunt Edith, your uncle Carl, and uncle Timothy. And of course Grandma and Grandpa Schmidt."

Frank couldn't remember his relatives very well, but they still received letters from them from time to time.

"Did people do bad things to you, Mama?" Frank asked.

Mama nodded. "They called us names and made fun of us. Sometimes we were just ignored. One time they threw a rock through our front-door window." She went on to explain how Germans lost their jobs and how German books were burned.

Frank was shocked. He never knew his mama had had to endure such things.

"But," he said, "at least they didn't put you into camps like they've done to the Japanese."

"No, thankfully," Mama agreed. "But there was talk of it."

"How did you stand it?"

"It was because your grandfather was such a good example to all of us children. Since he was president of his labor union, and since he was German, people falsely accused him of sabotaging the flour mill where he worked."

"Sabotage?" Frank said. "That's a serious accusation."

"So serious he was taken to jail. But only for one night."

"I bet he was fighting mad after that," Frank said.

Mama shook her head. "Not your grandfather. Of course he was angry at the senseless prejudice, but he never allowed anger to control him." She looked at Frank, and he squirmed. "Papa always told us children not to let hate overtake us. Because one day the war would be over and then what would we do with the hate inside of us? And now I want to teach that same thing to you."

She looked straight at Frank. "Your father has been an example to you. He knows he cannot erase all the hate in the land, but he made the decision to do what he could by taking care of the Fairfax while the Wakamutsus are being held. I hope you realize the sacrifice he has made. Be proud of him. But better yet, follow his example."

"Want to come with me?" Frank asked Eddie the next day.

"Yeah, sure." Then the younger boy added, "Where're you going?"

"To see a friend of mine."

Frank had been thinking of going to see Ronnie for several days but had put it off. After all the things Mama had said last evening, however, he was determined to go. He certainly owed Ronnie an apology.

First Frank called Mr. Wickard to get Ronnie's address. Then he and Eddie set out to find the apartment. It wasn't too hard. The apartment was above a shoe repair shop in the heart of the international district. It was a small apartment, in the back, facing the alley. After they'd found the place, it took all of Frank's courage just to knock on the door.

A man's voice answered, "Come on in. It's unlocked."

Frank stepped into a sparsely furnished, but clean living room with Eddie right behind him. A service flag hung in the double windows, and on top of the radio was a photo of a young man in uniform. That would be Ronnie's older brother, Martin.

A faded couch sat by the window, and an overstuffed chair with bits of stuffing coming out sat nearby. In the middle of the room, taking up most of the space, was a bed. A man, looking thin and frail, sat in the bed, propped up with several pillows behind his back. Just as Frank started to introduce himself, Ronnie came into the room.

"Well hello, Frank. I never thought I'd see you here." Turning to the man, he said, "Dad, this is the boy whose father took over the Fairfax for the Wakamutsus."

Mr. Denton's eyebrows went up. "Is that right? What an act of gallantry in the midst of this mixed-up old world," he said gently. "I know the Wakamutsus will be forever grateful."

Frank nodded. "Yes, sir. Thank you, sir. I've come over here to apologize to your son."

"Ah," said Mr. Denton. "Gallant like your father?"

"Not exactly," Frank admitted. "But I'm trying." Stumbling over his words, but determined to get it out, Frank apologized for his rudeness the day Ronnie asked him to join the ball team. "I was acting pretty stuck up, and I'm really sorry. I'd sure like to join that team if you're still needing someone."

A smile broke over Ronnie's face. "We'd love to have you." Then he added. "What about your brother there?"

"Eddie?" Frank said.

"Sure. Why not? We let several young guys join us. We figure the best way for them to learn is to get out there and play."

Frank thought about that. Looking down at Eddie's grinning face, he said, "I guess that's right. Well, Eddie what do you think?"

"Wow!"

"Practice is this afternoon at four," Ronnie explained. "At the school."

"We'll be there," Frank said. Stepping over to Mr. Denton, he shook the man's thin hand. "Pleased to have met you, sir."

It was like heaven to be back on the ball field. Frank was determined he wasn't going to shove his way into this group by showing off. He would play where he was told to play, which meant he was beside Eddie in the outfield. That pleased Eddie to no end. And just as Ronnie had told them, there were several boys Eddie's age in the game. All were having a great time.

That evening, Frank asked permission to wait up for Dad to come home from work. When Mama asked why, he just said he had to talk to him about something.

Dad looked rather surprised to come in at two in the morning and be met by a sleepy-eyed Frank sitting on the couch with a pile of comic books.

"Hey there, Frankie boy," he said smiling. "Are you my reception party tonight? What's up?"

Frank looked up, rubbing his eyes. "Hi, Dad. Can we talk a minute?"

"Sure. Come on into the kitchen. Let's have some Ovaltine and talk."

Dad set his lunch bucket on the cabinet. Opening the cupboard, he pulled out a sauce pan. From the fridge he took a bottle of milk and measured out two cups into the pan and turned on the burner on the stove. "How many spoons for you?"

"Two. Heaping."

Dad smiled. When two mugs of steaming Ovaltine were giving off a sweet chocolate scent, they sat down at the table together.

"Now, what's on your mind?" Dad asked.

Frank paused a minute, not sure how to start. Mittens

121

strolled in and rubbed against their legs, enjoying this late night company.

"There's this boy from school named Ronnie Denton," Frank began, then he went on to explain Ronnie's predicament and how his brother went off to war, the caring Japanese family was interned, and that Ronnie had to care for his invalid father all by himself.

Dad listened carefully, drank the rest of his Ovaltine, and then said, "That's an interesting story, Frank, but why are you telling me about it?"

Frank thought a minute. "Well, I thought maybe we could find a place for Ronnie and his dad here. At the Fairfax. The two of them wouldn't be alone anymore. They'd be around lots of caring folks. And you could hire Ronnie to help with the work around here as partial payment for the rent. What do you think? Could we do that?"

Dad was smiling. He reached out and put his big arm around Frank's shoulders. "I'm proud of you, Frank. Really proud of you."

Frank felt his face flush. "I haven't done anything yet. I'm just thinking about it."

"Well, I like the way you're thinking." Dad took the cups to the sink to rinse them out. "We don't have any apartments available right now, but we could move them over to one of the double rooms in the hotel. From there we could move them into the first apartment that opens up. How's that?"

"Swell."

Frank couldn't believe how great he felt. Better than anything he'd felt in a long, long time. He couldn't wait to tell Ronnie and Mr. Denton the news.

CHAPTER 16
Frank's Plan

Summer days at the Fairfax were so much better now that Ronnie was there. He and Frank read comics together, listened to radio programs, went to the movies, worked on model planes, and walked up Jackson Street to the school for shop class and ball practice. Frank was careful to include Eddie in their plans as much as he could. To Frank's surprise, Eddie wasn't nearly as big a pest as he used to be.

Alice somehow scrounged up a wheelchair for Mr. Denton. So instead of being confined to his room, he wheeled up and down the halls, talking to everyone. His eyes sparkled, and color returned to his cheeks. Frank was amazed at how much more alive he looked than he had the first day Frank met him.

Ronnie could work circles around Frank. There wasn't a job in the place that he wouldn't tackle at least once. Dad said that hiring Ronnie was one of the best business decisions he'd made since they took over the Fairfax.

Ronnie turned out to be a fair baseball player. Trouble was he'd never had the time to practice before, nor did he have anyone to show him the finer points of the game. Now that he didn't have to spend every spare minute watching over his father, there was more time to play ball. The Feinstein Hardware team was winning every game they played.

Letters from the Wakamutsus arrived regularly. And the Harringtons sent plenty of letters back, along with a special box of goodies, which was taken to Puyallup weekly by Pastor and Mrs. Hopkins. The couple drove to Puyallup every weekend to hold services for the people who had made up their church. Because his congregation couldn't pay him anymore, the pastor had to find a job to support himself. But he continued to minister to his people no matter where they had to be.

That, Frank thought, was a true "man of valor."

The Wakamutsus wrote about making do without all the luxuries of life, of dealing with monotony and boredom, and of wading through oceans of ankle-deep mud that appeared after every rain.

If it weren't for the spiritual encouragement we receive from the services each week, Mr. Wakamutsu wrote, *I'm not sure how we would survive.*

Yoshiko wrote about the open-air record concerts they had on Sunday afternoons:

We spread blankets out on the grass and they play phonograph records over a loudspeaker. For a moment or two, we can lie there listening to the music and relaxing, and almost forget where we are. It helps us get through the week.

Then she added, *I sure miss Mittens. And my phonograph player!*

Mr. Wakamutsu wrote that he and the boys were able to find pieces of lumber and hammer and nails and had built a makeshift table for their "stall" room, along with shelves that helped organize the clutter. *If you can imagine,* he wrote, *five people in a stall can be rather crowded!*

Kaneko wrote of the awful heat and how it made many of the older men irritable and short-tempered.

Many of the families here are not Christians, he wrote, *and the men have trigger-tempers. I try to stay out of their way.*

Time and again Frank recalled the day when the Wakamutsus left and he had run away. How silly he'd acted. And how ashamed he was.

They had known from the beginning that the time the Wakamutsus spent in Puyallup was temporary. The government's plan was to keep the Japanese in temporary holding areas until more permanent camps were ready. All through the summer, the Harringtons waited for news telling them that the interned Japanese would be moved from the fairgrounds to some undetermined place. No one knew when. And no one knew where.

Then, in the middle of August, the letter came. The Wakamutsus were being moved to Idaho.

"Idaho?" Isabel said in disbelief. "Why Idaho? There's nothing in Idaho."

125

They were in the living room listening to Mama read the letter.

Frank shared Isabel's question. Any pictures he had ever seen of Idaho were of wastelands and sagebrush. Frank thought of Kaneko and his love of nature, especially trees and flowers. How would he survive in such a barren setting?

All day long, after he'd heard the news, Frank thought about his friends leaving the state of Washington and going all the way to Idaho. How he wished he and his family could go to Puyallup before the Wakamutsus left. Surely there was a way.

First he went to Mama and asked her if they could drive to Puyallup. "Think of what a visit from all of us would mean to them," he said. "Especially at this time."

Mama shook her head. "I know it sounds like a good idea, Frank, but first of all, I don't think we have enough ration stamps for gas. And secondly, there's just too much work to do here for us to get away. And plus, your Dad is working days and can't drive us."

"You could drive us," he persisted. "If we had enough ration stamps, could we go?"

Mama paused. "I guess I could talk to Alice and see what she thinks about the idea."

Frank grabbed his mother's arm. "Let's both go talk to Alice." Frank knew his older sister well enough to know she'd be all in favor of the idea.

True to form, Alice said, "Well, of course you should go. I can take care of everything here. Remember, Ronnie's here to help now. Leave the twins with me, and you take Frank and Audrey and Isabel. Why," she added, "just think what that would mean to Mr. and Mrs. Wakamutsu."

"My very words," Frank said with a smile and a wink to his oldest sister.

Frank was overjoyed when they rounded up just enough ration stamps to put gas in the car for the drive to Puyallup. The evening before their trip, he rode along with Alice to the filling station to get gas.

"It feels strange to be behind the wheel again," she said as she drove away from the Fairfax. "I miss not being able to jump in the car and go someplace anytime we want."

"Me, too," Frank agreed.

"Remember when we used to go on Sunday drives?" she said with a tinge of wistfulness in her voice. "Dad would drive, and we'd go anywhere and nowhere—seeing new sights and enjoying the scenery along the way. And we could go along at a pretty good lick, too, not like the limit of thirty-five miles per hour that we have to follow now."

"I remember," he said, although he had to work really hard to picture the drives Alice described. He'd put those pleasant memories way back in his mind. He could hardly think of a time when Dad had had time to go for a leisurely drive, let alone have gas enough to do it.

Alice steered the car into the corner filling station a few blocks from the Fairfax. A teenaged boy came out to the car dressed in a filling-station attendant's uniform. Frank thought of Steve and winced as the pain of his brother's absence swept over him.

The boy said, "Fill 'er up?" and grinned.

It was a good joke, since hardly anyone could fill up their tanks these days. Alice chuckled as she dug in her purse for the ration stamps. She handed him the stamps, and between the two of them, they figured out how many gallons could be purchased.

While the gas pump was running, the boy lifted the hood and checked the oil, then washed the windshield. After the gas was paid for and Alice was driving out of the station, she said to Frank, "I'm so glad you thought of this trip. It's going to be nice for the Wakamutsus, but it's also going to be good for Mama. She really needs to get away."

"She does?" Frank felt a little guilty that he'd not thought of that before.

"She's hardly had one break since we moved. This will be good for her," Alice said.

Frank started to point out to Alice that she, too, was working hard and she, too, hadn't had a day off, but he figured she knew that better than he did. So he kept quiet. Mama said once that Alice buried herself in work in order to keep her sanity. It was hard enough for Frank to deal with Jim being missing. He couldn't imagine how Alice must feel. She was engaged to the guy, after all.

Sitting in the car with his sister, Frank determined that he was going to try to think of special things to do for Alice. Something that might help to cheer her up. He'd been so full of his own problems that he'd paid scant attention to Mama or Alice. That was going to change.

The next morning, Audrey, Isabel, Frank, and Mama were getting things loaded for the trip. They wanted to take as many "goodies" as they could. Frank made sure he had new comic books for the boys, as well as fresh sketch paper and ink for Kaneko. Even though Kodak film was in short supply, they'd taken photos of Mittens and had them developed as a surprise for Yoshiko.

The boxes and sacks were full of fruits and nuts and candy bars, as well as some of Mama's homemade cookies. Frank had added several packages of bubble gum. While bubble gum was getting as scarce as sugar, Frank wanted the boys to have it. Even Eddie was willing to give up a couple packages of his bubble gum, which Frank knew was a big sacrifice.

Yoshiko mentioned in one of her letters how much she needed a pair of galoshes for walking in all that mud and rain. Due to the rubber shortage, the Harringtons hadn't been able to find any galoshes in all Seattle. Isabel decided to give her red ones away to Yoshiko. "After all," she told Mama, "we have sidewalks in Seattle. All Yoshiko has is mud."

When everything was loaded, Mama got into the car and pushed her foot down on the starter, expecting the DeSoto to fire off as it always did. But the engine whined a few times and then silence. Again she turned the key. Nothing.

CHAPTER 17

To Puyallup

"Someone's siphoned our gas," Mama said with a sigh of resignation.

"What?" Frank almost yelled. "Who would do such a thing?"

"A lot of people would do such a thing," Mama said. "Someone probably saw you and Alice go to the filling station last night. All they had to do was wait until dark, and they had extra gas. It happens all the time now that gas is so precious."

Frank was fuming mad. "Of all the nerve."

"I guess this trip wasn't such a good idea after all," Mama said, opening her door to get out.

"Oh yes, it *is* a good idea. And we're still going."

"It's too late to try to get the bus," Isabel said.

"We're taking the car," Frank told them. "Come on, let's go to the kitchen and pull out all the ration stamps we have. Then we're going around to all our friends in the apartments and in the neighborhood and trade our stamps for gas stamps."

Mama looked at him a minute as though she thought he were a little crazy. "Do you know what you're saying, Frank? That means we may have to go without our sugar ration and shortening and who knows what all else."

"That's nothing compared to what the Wakamutsus are having to do without," Frank countered.

Audrey spoke up in her soft voice. "Frank's right, Mama. Whatever we give up will be worth it."

Mama looked at Isabel. "Do you agree?"

Isabel nodded. "I totally agree! Even with our shortages we have so much more than the Wakamutsus."

It was settled. The next half hour was spent in a frenzy of stamp trading and then regrouping to see what they had gained. Frank put the gas stamps down on the table. "We're almost there," he said. "We only need a few more." They scurried out again to trade more stamps until they were certain they had enough stamps for the gas to get from Seattle to Puyallup and back again.

Frank had to run to the station and fill a gas can with gas just so they could get the car started. Then, waving good-bye to Alice and the twins, they drove to the filling station, purchased the needed gas, and were on their way.

The girls agreed to sit in the back seat where they could chatter to their hearts' content. That meant Frank had to sit up front with Mama. But that didn't bother him one bit. When the whole family went anywhere together, Frank hardly ever got to sit up front. There was a much better view of the road, and it had been so long since he'd been outside the city, that he'd almost forgotten what the country looked like.

Alice was right about Mama needing a break. She was dressed up in her Sunday hat with the flowers and veil, and her nice blue polka-dot dress, with her white pumps and gloves. The tired look she'd been wearing lately seemed to evaporate as they drove along. And no one even cared that they couldn't drive any faster than thirty-five miles an hour.

Their jovial mood lasted until they drove up to the state fairgrounds. When they saw the sight before them, they could hardly speak for the shock. Even though they talked to Pastor and Mrs. Hopkins regularly and even though the couple had told them of the awful conditions, Frank realized a person had to see it to truly understand.

Tall chain fences stood around the outside of the fairgrounds, and armed soldiers patrolled the fences. At the corners of the fences were high towers where soldiers armed with tommy guns kept twenty-four-hour vigil. Pastor Hopkins told them that at night, powerful searchlights swept relentlessly back and forth, back and forth. Did they really worry that someone might try to escape? Frank wondered. Where would a Japanese person go? It was impossible to hide the Japanese appearance of their faces.

Inside the fences, Frank watched hundreds of Japanese-Americans coming and going from one building to another. In addition to the existing buildings, rows of makeshift buildings had been thrown together. They looked almost like rows of chicken houses. These, too, Frank knew from Pastor Hopkins's reports, were homes for the displaced Japanese families.

Frank sat and stared. What would it be like to be inside there and know you could not leave? No matter how much you wanted to, you could never leave.

Why were these innocent people fenced in and guarded? What had happened to the American system to allow such an unfair thing to take place? Yoshiko, Kaneko, and Abiko Wakamutsu had all been born in America. They were American citizens as much as Frank was. How could they be imprisoned without a fair trial? Suddenly he wasn't sure he could stand to go inside and see his friends in such a horrible place.

Mama's face was grim as she pulled into a nearby parking lot and parked the car under a shade tree.

"I know this is not going to be easy," she said, "but we have a job to do here. And that job is to encourage our friends and lighten their load as much as possible." Glancing over at Frank, she added, "We knew it was going to be a sacrifice to come. Now you're going to understand how much of a sacrifice it truly is."

Frank could see that he hadn't thought this project through to the end. All he'd thought of was coming to see the Wakamutsus and bringing good things. He never thought of how appalling it would be to actually see the place.

"Come on," Isabel said. "I can't wait to see Yoshiko!"

They climbed out of the car and went around to the trunk, where they gathered the sacks and boxes of goodies. The guards let them in through the gate and led them into a waiting area in one of the exhibit buildings. Chairs and tables were scattered here and there throughout the large room, which had a concrete floor. They picked out a table and gratefully placed their pack-ages on it. Then they pulled up enough chairs around it for all of them to be able to sit. There they waited. The guards would let the Wakamutsus know that they had visitors. Other families were in the visiting center talking in low voices to those who'd cared enough to come for a visit.

Suddenly there was a loud squeal. It was Yoshiko. "Isabel!" she yelled. "I can't believe it! It's really you!"

The two girls ran to give each other a big hug and then spun round and round, laughing and crying. Entering behind Yoshiko walked Mr. and Mrs. Wakamutsu. They didn't move quite as fast as they used to. Frank was shocked to see Mrs. Wakamutsu dressed in a pair of slacks and wearing a head scarf over her black hair. In Seattle, she would never have worn a pair of slacks, and when she went out of the hotel, she was never without her nice hat and a pair of matching gloves. *How difficult this must be for such a fine lady,* Frank thought.

Mr. and Mrs. Wakamutsu bowed low to Mama and then shook her hand, murmuring their thanks to her for coming.

"I am so sorry," Mrs. Wakamutsu said. "I cannot even offer you one little cup of tea."

Mama laughed. "We've already bought bottles of soda pop from the vendor. Come on over to the table. We can eat from the things we've brought."

Mr. Wakamutsu looked over at Audrey and Frank. He smiled. Pointing to the door they'd just entered, he said, "The boys are on their way."

Frank and Audrey ran across the room to the door. A nearby soldier prevented them from going out onto the fairgrounds, but they could see Kaneko and Abiko coming toward them on a dead run.

"Frank! Audrey!" they shouted. "Hello!"

Suddenly the boys were there. Frank's best friends. He could hardly believe it. They shook hands, slapped shoulders. Both boys gave Audrey a hug.

"This is unbelievable," Kaneko said. "Why didn't you tell us you were coming?"

"There wasn't time," Frank said, laughing. "We just decided a day or so ago."

"And then someone siphoned our gas," Audrey put in. "So we almost didn't get to come after all."

Frank changed the subject quickly because he didn't want the boys to know all the stamps they traded just to get there.

"Come on over and say hi to Mama and Isabel," he said, "then look at the stuff we brought."

"Wow," Abiko said, "you brought more? You always send so much to us each week. Getting your packages is like Christmas every week."

"Hey," Frank said, "it's nothing. What are friends for, anyway?"

Suddenly Abiko was laughing. "Look at Yoshiko," he said, pointing.

Yoshiko was wearing Isabel's red galoshes and dancing the jitterbug like she'd gone nutty. "Galoshes! Galoshes!" she sang as she danced.

Her parents were trying to shush her, but it did no good.

"This is so wonderful," she said laughing. "Do you *know* how muddy this place gets when it rains? Never in my life have I ever seen so much mud."

No one ever let on that those were Isabel's galoshes. They didn't want the Wakamutsus to feel badly. Frank figured that Mr. and Mrs. Wakamutsu would probably return the gift if they knew the galoshes belonged to Isabel.

"There's more," Isabel said. "Look at this, Yoshiko!" She handed her friend the pictures of Mittens.

Yoshiko's eyes filled with tears. "At least you're taking good care of her. Many of the families here had to have their pets put to sleep or give them over to strangers. They will never see their cats and dogs again."

Kaneko was thrilled over the sketch books, and both boys were excited about new comics and packages of bubble gum.

After the initial excitement had worn down, everyone sat around the table, eating nuts from the packages, drinking bottles of cold soda pop, and talking. Mr. Wakamutsu told how he had been elected as one of the block leaders. Mrs. Wakamutsu was teaching lessons in doll making to the younger girls. And Yoshiko had a job in the personnel department, keeping records of people's work hours.

"It's so silly," Yoshiko told them in a low voice so the guards couldn't hear, "but we cannot even go from one building to another without armed chaperones. What do they think we're going to do? Do they truly have enough spare soldiers so they can afford to keep such close watch over all of us?"

When Mama asked how many Japanese were at the fairgrounds, Mr. Wakamutsu told her there were about ten thousand. "That's not counting all the other camps up and down the West Coast," he added sadly. "But we hope our cooperation will prove to people how much we love this country."

"There are rabble-rousers in here as well," Mrs. Wakamutsu said in her quiet voice.

"What kind of rabble-rousers?" Isabel asked.

"The kind who truly want Japan to win the war," Mr. Wakamutsu said, lowering his voice still further. "Some of them are counting the days till their countrymen land and come ashore to set them free.

"One of the bad things about gathering so many people in one place," he continued, "is that you end up mixing all the bad in with all the good. It's not a well-thought-out plan. Not at all."

"That's why Papa wanted to be a block leader," Kaneko put in. "He hopes he can help keep the rabble-rousers quiet and keep things on an even keel."

If anyone could do that, Frank was sure Mr. Wakamutsu could.

As they visited, the Wakamutsus told stories about the food that was so different from what they were used to eating, noise from neighbors in the adjoining stalls, the leaky roof, and the horrible latrines. But they made the stories funny, and to his surprise, Frank found himself laughing out loud. Guiltily, he remembered how stubborn he'd been when he learned he had to move from Queen Anne Hill. He never once tried to see the bright side of the situation. Not at first anyway. He sure had a lot to learn.

Much too soon, it was time to leave. Mama offered a prayer of protection over their friends while they lived in Idaho, and she thanked God for their friendships. Mr. Wakamutsu closed the prayer by praying blessings over the Harringtons as well.

"We can walk you to the front door," Mrs. Wakamutsu said as they stood up from the table. Smiling, she added, "But we can't go out to the parking lot."

Over and over the Wakamutsus thanked the Harringtons for the visit and for bringing the wonderful gifts to them. And silly Yoshiko kept dancing around, the red galoshes still on her feet.

Hanging back just a little, Frank draped his arm about

Kaneko's shoulder. "Kaneko," he said, "there's something I want to say to you. You, too, Abiko."

"When you left in April, just like a little kid I went running off—"

"Hey," Abiko interrupted. "You don't need to apologize for that. We knew how you were hurting for us."

Frank nodded. "I know, but I never got to tell you." He swallowed hard and started again. "I never got a chance to tell you. . ." His voice cracked. "The two of you are my very best friends. And I don't care what anyone in the whole world says about you. They can take you to the farthest corner of the earth, but you will never stop being my best friends."

Then, just like the day with Eddie in the supply closet, Frank started crying. He buried his face in Kaneko's shoulder. Kaneko was hanging onto him, and Abiko came up and hugged the two of them. All three of them were in tears. Then Audrey joined them, and she was crying as well.

"Would you look at that!" Yoshiko said, kidding them. "You'd have thought it would be Isabel and me crying." Then she turned to hug Isabel, and in a minute they, too, were in tears.

None of them knew how long it would be before they saw one another again. War, it seemed to Frank, was one long series of good-byes.

CHAPTER 18

Father, Forgive Them

Lost in their own private thoughts, the Harringtons didn't talk much as Mama drove back to Seattle. It had been a bittersweet reunion, but in spite of everything, Frank was thankful that he'd at last been able to express his feelings. As he watched the wooded hills passing by the car window, he rubbed his knuckles and thought how much better it felt to weep with his friends than to vent his anger in a fist fight.

Since Dad was working the day shift, they were all together at supper that evening. He smiled as they told and retold the stories of the day. They all laughed at the thought of Yoshiko dancing about in her red galoshes, not caring who was watching.

"I wish I could have seen her," Barb said. "She must have been so happy."

"I'm proud of you," Dad said to Isabel, "for your generosity. You know that we may not be able to get you another pair for a very long time."

Isabel nodded. "I know. But it was worth it."

Frank had to agree. Even now, crowded around the table in the small dining room, it was worth it to be able to keep the business together for the Wakamutsus. He would do his part to make sure his friends had a home to come back to after the war. It was worth everything he'd had to give up. And now as he thought back, he realized it hadn't been all that much.

That night, after they had gone to bed, Eddie hung his head over the side of the upper bunk. In the dim light, Frank could see his face.

"Frank?" he said.

"Yeah?"

"Audrey told me something."

"What did she tell you, Eddie?"

"She said you cried when it was time to leave Kaneko and Abiko." He paused a minute. "Is that right? Did you?"

"Hm mm. You heard right."

"Why did you cry?"

Frank felt his eyes getting all misty again just thinking about the moment. "Because I care a lot about those guys."

"Frank?"

"Yeah."

"You cried that day with me. When you found me in the closet with all the mops."

"That's right. I did."

140

Eddie's head was hanging down a little farther, and his face was getting red from being upside down. "Did that mean you care about me?"

"Of course, I care about you, Eddie. I care about you a lot."

There was silence for a moment. "Sometimes I feel like you don't," Eddie said at last.

Frank winced at the remark. He knew why Eddie felt that way. It was because Frank hadn't been a very good big brother. Not at all like Steve. "Well, I do care," he said. But he knew it was going to take more than words.

"Frank?"

"Yeah."

"Can I come down there for a while?"

"Sure, why not?"

"Boy, oh boy!"

With a quick vault, down he came. Frank moved over so his back was up against the wall, and he let Eddie lay his head on Frank's arm. Frank gave him a gentle Dutch rub on his head and then laughed.

For a time they lay there talking about the upcoming baseball game. Frank explained the different rules and plays that Eddie didn't understand too well.

Just then, Eddie reached up to the mattress above them. "What's that sticking out there?" he asked. "Is that something of yours?"

"Now why would I stick anything of mine in your mattress?" Frank asked.

Together they got out of bed and lifted up the mattress. Pressed between the mattress and the bed springs was a drawing. One of Kaneko's pen-and-ink drawings.

"Get the light, Eddie. Let's take a better look." As the light came on, Frank sat down on the edge of the bed, gently cradling the drawing in his hands. "Would you look at this," he breathed.

Eddie sat down beside him as they studied the sketch together. In the upper lefthand background was a Japanese flag and a likeness of Emperor Hirohito. In the other corner was the Stars and Stripes and a likeness of President Roosevelt. The foreground showed a scene of Japanese-Americans being forced to leave their homes and businesses.

The caption written in Kaneko's swirling pen strokes read: "Father, forgive them. They know not what they do."

Eddie stared at the picture. "How can he do that, Frank? How can he forgive people who caused him to have to live in an animal stall at the fairgrounds?"

"Only with God, Eddie. Only with God."

"Let's go show Mama and Dad."

Frank placed the treasured drawing on the desk next to his model airplanes. "Tomorrow, Eddie. We'll show it to them tomorrow."

Frank was already planning how he would mount the drawing in a very special frame. Every day he would look at it and remember. Remember that he must be brave. Brave like the Wakamutsu family. Brave like Jim, missing in action in the Pacific. Brave like Steve, learning to drive tanks somewhere in England. Brave like Dad, who wasn't afraid to give up his home to help his friends. And yes, brave like Grandpa Schmidt, who had determined never to allow anger and bitterness rule his life.

While Frank knew he still wasn't yet a "mighty man of valor," he sure wanted to be in the running. And each day he was getting closer.

Gently, he put his arm around Eddie, who was now snuggled next to him, and slowly drifted off to sleep.

There's More!

The American Adventure continues with *The Home Front*. Barb and Eddie Harrington are suspicious. Sal Bolella says he works at a shipyard, but when he's supposed to be working, they see him on the street, talking with strangers.

Then he finds out that their dad works at Boeing and starts quizzing them about the planes that are being built. Everyone knows that you don't discuss bomber designs during a war. Why is he trying to get the twins to spill secrets?

Sal says he's a welder, but his clothes always have red stains on them. Is Sal who he says he is? And if he isn't a welder, what's he really trying to do in Seattle?

You're in for the ultimate
American Adventure!
Collect all 48 books!

The Plymouth Period (1620-1634)
1) *The Mayflower Adventure*
   ISBN 1-57748-059-7
2) *Plymouth Pioneers*
   ISBN 1-57748-060-0
3) *Dream Seekers* ISBN 1-57748-073-2

The Boston Period (1635-1808)
4) *Fire by Night* ISBN 1-57748-074-0
5) *Queen Anne's War*
   ISBN 1-57748-146-1
6) *Danger in the Harbor*
   ISBN 1-57748-147-X
7) *Smallpox Strikes!* ISBN 1-57748-144-5
8) *Maggie's Choice* ISBN 1-57748-145-3
9) *Boston Revolts!* ISBN 1-57748-156-9
10) *The Boston Massacre*
   ISBN 1-57748-157-7
11) *The American Revolution*
   ISBN 1-57748-158-5
12) *The American Victory*
   ISBN 1-57748-159-3
13) *Adventure in the Wilderness*
   ISBN 1-57748-230-1

The Cincinnati Period (1808-1865)
14) *Earthquake in Cincinnati*
   ISBN 1-57748-231-X
15) *Trouble on the Ohio River*
   ISBN 1-57748-232-8
16) *Escape from Slavery*
   ISBN 1-57748-233-6
17) *Cincinnati Epidemic*
   ISBN 1-57748-255-7
18) *Riot in the Night* ISBN 1-57748-256-5
19) *Fight for Freedom*
   ISBN 1-57748-257-3
20) *Enemy or Friend?*
   ISBN 1-57748-258-1
21) *Danger on the Railroad*
   ISBN 1-57748-259-X
22) *Time for Battle* ISBN 1-57748-260-3
23) *The Rebel Spy* ISBN 1-57748-267-0
24) *War's End* ISBN 1-57748-268-9

The Minneapolis Period (1876-1935)
25) *Centennial Celebration*
   ISBN 1-57748-287-5
26) *The Great Mill Explosion*
   ISBN 1-57748-288-3
27) *Lights for Minneapolis*
   ISBN 1-57748-289-1
28) *The Streetcar Riots*
   ISBN 1-57748-290-5
29) *Chicago World's Fair*
   ISBN 1-57748-291-3
30) *A Better Bicycle* ISBN 1-57748-292-1
31) *The New Citizen*
   ISBN 1-57748-392-8
32) *The San Francisco Earthquake*
   ISBN 1-57748-393-6
33) *Marching with Sousa*
   ISBN 1-57748-406-1
34) *Clash with the Newsboys*
   ISBN 1-57748-407-X
35) *Prelude to War*
   ISBN 1-57748-410-X
36) *The Great War* ISBN 1-57748-411-8
37) *The Flu Epidemic*
   ISBN 1-57748-451-7
38) *Women Win the Vote*
   ISBN 1-57748-452-5
39) *Battling the Klan*
   ISBN 1-57748-453-3
40) *The Bootlegger Menace*
   ISBN 1-57748-454-1
41) *Black Tuesday* ISBN 1-57748-474-6
42) *The Great Depression*
   ISBN 1-57748-475-4

The Seattle Period (1935-1945)
43) *Starting Over* ISBN 1-57748-509-2
44) *Changing Times* ISBN 1-57748-510-6
45) *Rumblings of War*
   ISBN 1-57748-511-4
46) *War Strikes* ISBN 1-57748-512-2
47) *The Home Front* ISBN 1-57748-513-0
48) *Coming Home* ISBN 1-57748-514-9